The MYSTERY FANcier

This issue is dedicated to the memory of

Larry French

who died this past December in an automobile accident. Larry is the first of our number to leave our ranks through death. He will be remembered for his many reviews and articles for TMF; for his apazine *Cuprit Confesses* in DAPA-EM; for his great enthusiasm for and work on his favorite mystery writer, John Dickson Carr; and, by me at least, for his kindness and generosity and--most remarkable of all--his ability to accept criticism gracefully. *The MYSTERY FANcier* is poorer for his having left us.

Volume 3 Number 1

March April 1979

THE MYSTERY FANCIER

Volume 3 Number 1
January/February 1979

TABLE OF CONTENTS

MYSTERIOUSLY SPEAKING 1
Gene Stratton-Porter: Mistress of the Mini-Mystery,
    by Jane S. Bakerman 3
The Len Deighton Series, by Jeff Banks and Harry Dawson . . 10
Kim Philby, Master Spy in Fact and Fiction,
    by Theodore P. Dukeshire. 14
Bouchercon, 1978: IX and Counting, by Donald A. Yates . . . 15
The Nero Wolfe Saga, Part XI, by Guy M. Townsend. 21
An Index of Books Reviewed in TMF Volume 2,
    Compiled by David H. Doerrer. 26
MYSTERY*FILE: Short Reviews by Steve Lewis. 31
VERDICTS (More Reviews) 38
THE DOCUMENTS IN THE CASE (Letters) 46

The MYSTERY FANcier
is edited and published bi-monthly by Guy M. Townsend,
1120 Bluebird Lane, Memphis, Tennessee 38116, U.S.A.
Contributions of all descriptions are welcomed. Deadline for the March/April 1979 issue: 15 February 1979.

SUBSCRIPTION RATES: Domestic second class mail, $9.00 per year (6 issues); Overseas surface mail, $9.00; Overseas airmail, $12.00. Overseas subscribers please pay in international money order, check drawn on U. S. bank, or currency; no checks drawn on foreign banks, please. Make checks payable to Guy M. Townsend, not *The MYSTERY FANcier*.

Second class postage paid at Memphis, Tennessee

Copyright 1979 by Guy M. Townsend
All rights reserved for contributors
ISSN: 0146-3160

MYSTERIOUSLY SPEAKING . . .

As was the case last year, subscription renewals are slow to come in. About half have renewed as of this writing and will receive this issue in the second class mailing. Those who renew late will receive their copies via book rate mail or first class--either way, it's going to cost me an extra $40-50. Next year I'm going to explicitly state that there will be a $1.00 penalty for late renewals.

On the subject of renewals, several of you renewed your subscriptions at the $7.50 rate, choosing to disregard the price increase, while others complained that the subscription rate was said to be $9.00 in the editorial but $7.50 on the contents page. It's really quite simple, folks: the previous issue was the last issue of volume two, for which the subscription rate was $7.50. Therefore, the contents page showed the rate under which that issue fell. The new rate went into effect with this issue and so was mentioned in the editorial. Simple.

Several of the people who should have received credit for letters of comment in volume two declined to take credit and sent in the full amount, choosing in that fashion to demonstrate their belief that letters should not be credited against subscription costs. For my part, I think that a letter is as much a contribution as a review, and some letters are even more significant contributions than some articles, so next year, folks, I hope that you will take the credits which you certainly have earned.

Volume one is nearly out of print. Numbers one through four are entirely exhausted and I have only a few copies of five and six left. The Preview Issue is also out of print. Some of you late-joiners missed out on these early issues, and it is virtually certain that I will never have time to reissue them in the future. For the really fanatical completist, however, I do offer a solution, albeit an expensive one. I will loan out my file copies of these out of print issues for people to xerox on their own under certain conditions: that they send me $4.00 to cover the cost of first class postage and insurance to them (the actual cost is almost exactly $3.00, if the minimum amount of insurance is used, but my file copies are worth a damned sight more than $15.00 so I'm going to insist on more insurance); that they agree to keep them no longer than one week (so that I can get them back to send on to others who want to copy them); that they agree to mail them back to me via insured first class mail; and that they treat them as gently as possible while they have custody of them. I will do this for as long as it takes the post office to lose the copies (which, given the p.o.'s track record, probably won't be long). Before you leap to take me up on this, think about how much it is likely to cost you. Helen Weber xeroxed these four issues and it cost her $22.00. Add $8.00 for two way postage and insurance and you get $30.00, or $7.50 per number. More than a little steep, I'd say, but that's up to you.

As you will see within, Don Yates finally came through with his Bouchercon report, which I have illustrated with a few snap shots I made in Chicago. I have no idea how the photographs will reproduce, particularly since they aren't very good to start with. Since Bouchercon I have learned a bit more about taking pictures, so my photos from next year's gathering should be much better. Before leaving the subject of Don's report I should inform you that when I received the manuscript it was accompanied by a limerick bad enough to make Ogden Nash blanch. Don has a great deal to answer for.

I have to 'fess up to something--I cannot take credit for the high quality of reproduction on the last issue (Joe Lansdale's critical remarks notwithstanding, I think that issue was the most readable yet). The fact is, I had it printed commercially. Here are the grim details. I thought I had more or less gotten the hang of both the plate maker and the offset press after doing 2:5, so I approached 2:6 with a fair degree of confidence. Which proved to be entirely without foundation. I set aside a weekend to run off the issues: Friday night for making plates, Saturday for running off the sheets, and Sunday for collating and stapling (it's just barely possible to do all that on a weekend, if you are willing to put in about 30 hours at a dead run). Friday night, then, I dragged out the old plate maker . . . and botched up half a dozen one dollar aluminum plates in a row. Better wait until tomorrow, I thought, and so I did. Only tomorrow wasn't much better. In fact, what with this and that, it was Sunday evening before I managed to get all thirty-odd plates finished, and by then I was having difficulty hanging on to the last vestiges of my sanity. I really intended to try to run off the copies Monday and Tuesday nights but I couldn't find the time and by the time the next weekend rolled around all the plates had oxidized and were worthless --another thirty plus dollars shot to hell. And to top it all off I managed to screw up one of the ink rollers on my offset press. After a couple hours of stomping around the house yelling and screaming a stream of curses that would have made a sailor's adam's apple bobble, I calmed down enough to telephone a friend in the printing business and asked him if he would print tha and subsequent issues for me, which he agreed to do. I managed to unload the offset equipment without taking too bad a bath, and now, for the first time in two and a half years, I am completely without duplicating equipment. And I feel like a newly freed slave. I have much more free time--all of which immediately filled up with additional activities, however--although I did have to cancel my order for the Silver Cloud I was going to pay for with the proceeds from this year's subscriptions. Oh well, easy come, easy go . . . .

Last issue's cover, by the way, was done by Dave Doerrer's wife. I can't find Dave's letter right now, but he said that it illustrated a mystery and he wondered if anyone would know which one.

As for this issue's cover, I would have used art if I had had any, and would have put the cover item in this column. Maybe, though, it's better this way. Larry will be missed.

2

GENE STRATTON-PORTER:
MISTRESS OF THE MINI-MYSTERY

By Jane S. Bakerman

I

Gene Stratton-Porter (1863-1924), one of the most popular American novelists of this century, stated flatly that she wrote fiction in order to support her nature books,[1] and she took great pride in her confidence that the novels provided sound and uplifting moral precepts.[2] In order to serve both her interest and her sense of duty, Stratton-Porter conceived a formula which made "moral" lessons and nature lore, both of which she loved to incorporate into her fiction, not only palatable but even attractive to her readers, great numbers of whom were children and adolescents.[3]

The first ingredient in the Stratton-Porter formula for popularization is predictable enough; generous dollops of love story were incorporated into each plot, and certainly these additions contributed to the books' success. A less usual means of doctoring the lessons in nature and in living, however, was her practice of embedding crime tales and mini-mysteries into her novels. This pattern holds true for the widely known *Freckles* (1904; Grosset & Dunlap, 1916) and *A Girl of the Limberlost* (1909; Grosset & Dunlap, n.d.) as well as for titles less well known today. *Laddie* (Garden City, New York: Doubleday, Page and Co., 1913), *Michael O'Halloran* (1915; New York: Grosset & Dunlap, 1916), *Her Father's Daughter* (Garden City, New York: Doubleday, Page and Co., 1921), *The White Flag* (Garden City, New York: Doubleday, Page and Co., 1923), and *The Keeper of the Bees* (1925; New York: Grosset & Dunlap, 1925) are examples which span her career and which include both major "divisions" of her fiction, the Indiana and the California novels. In a sense, the nature lore satisfied Stratton-Porter; the moralizing satisfied adults, often the *purchasers* of books for youngsters, and the mysteries and crime stories satisfied her young readers.

The plots of Stratton-Porter's novels are widely varied. *Freckles* and *A Girl of the Limberlost* are stories of wilderness youngsters whose natural ability and perseverance win them high places in society. *Laddie* recounts the adventures of a large Indiana family whose love for one another, high moral standards, and religious fervor make them examples of goodness and success to their neighbors. *Michael O'Halloran's* hero, Mickey, is a slum kid whose intelligence and street wisdom combine to make him not only a champion newsboy but also the fit guardian of a crippled orphan girl. *Her Father's Daughter* reports the maturation of Linda Strong, a teen-aged California naturalist whose clean heart and strong will enable her to find success and romance despite severe family troubles. *The White Flag* tells the love story of Mahala Spellman and Jason Peters and teaches readers that purity is all. *The Keeper of the Bees*, published posthumously, depicts wounded veteran Jamie MacFarlane's struggle back to health, during which he discovers a worthy career and finds a mate.

Diverse as the central plots are, however, the novels are strikingly alike because of the incorporation of the moral and the nature lessons, and especially because of the use of the crime tales and mini-mysteries which lend tension, suspense, and excitement to the plots. The combination yields the Stratton-Porter tone: sweetness and wholesomeness overlying straight sensationalism.

The sensationalism stems directly from the use of those crime tales and mini-mysteries, for though she incorporates these elements to spice the plots, she does not allow their inherent violence to be subordinated to puzzle or suspense as do most good mystery and detective novelists. Instead, she merely reports off-stage detection and *always* relies upon amazing coincidence to unsnarl the complications and to set the world to rights. Stratton-Porter's concern for the moral well being of her young audience did not prevent her from writing about dozens of acts of crime and violence in order to achieve sensational effects, and these crimes are important to the novels.

II

Ranging from breaking and entering to murder, the crime tales trigger plot complications and subplots, provide characterizations, and serve some of Stratton-Porter's basic themes. These crime tales are sometimes introduced rather abruptly and frequently are not resolved. The evil Morelands try to blackmail Mahala Spellman into marrying Junior Moreland (*Flag*, pp. 269-285), but the episode seems almost gratuitous and is hardly worthy of their capacity for villainy. Though the fact that Jamie MacFarlane is absent without leave from the army is excitingly stressed at the opening of the story (*Bees*, p. 10), it's forgotten after about fifty pages, and it certainly isn't allowed to shadow the happy ending. And in *A Girl of the Limberlost*, the early hints of rape and aborted thefts stop summarily when the love story takes over to provide interest (pp. 52-54).

Others of the crime tales are better integrated into the books, however. Sometimes, they provide foreshadowing as when Martin Moreland commits burglary to steal incriminating records (*Flag*, pp. 167-168). In *Laddie*, the theft of monies the Stanton family is holding for the county and for the church not only allows one son a brief chance to play detective but also foreshadows the solution of another mystery. Here, Stratton-Porter rather neatly enhances both the main and the subplots, achieves brisk characterization for Leon, the boy detective, and unifies her highly episodic plot (pp. 254-289).

Other crime tales also serve purposes of characterization— Jamie MacFarlane's defeat of a pair of roadside robbers testifies to his courage and tenacity (*Bees*, pp. 18-21). One of the most important of the several crimes appearing in *The White Flag* is perjury when Junior Moreland frames Mahala Spellman for theft. The device complicates the plot, of course, but primarily it is designed to show that Junior is irredeemably bad and that Mahala's decency and honor sustain her under any circumstance (pp. 355-371).

At times, crime is the central complication of the main plot, as in *Freckles*, perhaps Stratton-Porter's strongest use of the crime tale. Freckles achieves upward mobility because he successfully prevents the theft of valuable trees from the Limberlost (pp. 131-153). At other times, Stratton-Porter uses her crime tales to trigger an entire subplot, as in *Her Father's Daughter*. The theft of a set of house plans designed for a prestigious competition threatens the budding career of Marian Thorne; this story is the chief subplot for the novel and is not resolved until the heroine, Linda Strong, solves the mystery (pp. 31-376).

But crime tales are most intriguingly employed when Stratton-Porter presents them as supportive evidence for her basic themes. While the themes themselves may be suspect, and while the crime tales may be baldly sensational, their combination proved effective for great numbers of readers.

In novel after novel, Stratton-Porter stresses the importance of both heredity and environment in the development of a noble character, some novels stressing one, some stressing the other. *Her Father's Daughter* contrasts Linda and Eileen Strong, orphans. Linda, the product of her father's genes as well as of his tutelage in clean living and reverance for the out-of-doors, is steadily revealed as able, inventive, self-confident, and talented. Eileen, on the other hand, is vain, shallow, and self-seeking to the point of embezzling a major portion of Linda's inheritance (p. 311). To underscore her theory that the child of decent parents could hardly be so corrupt, Stratton-Porter reveals that the girls are not sisters, and that Eileen is the result not only of her mother's bad training but also of a tainted family background (pp. 314-315). Readers are allowed a ray of hope when Stratton-Porter suggests that Eileen may reform, guided by Linda's sterling example (pp. 467-471).

The influence of false values upon children is also heavily stressed in *Michael O'Halloran* in which Mickey, impoverished but of good stock and formed by good training, is contrasted with the Minturn boys, products of their mother's wrong ideas. The point is rammed home when Nellie Minturn's willingness to dismiss her children into the keeping of an exploitative French governess results in such severe child abuse that her little daughter is actually killed by the servant. Stratton-Porter exercises unusual skill in this crime tale, for the facts are reported by Mickey who has witnessed the incident, and his natural indignation coupled with the innocence of his point of view partially subordinate the sensationalism and underline the pathos (pp. 104-109).

Less tasteful, however, is the treatment of a second important theme in *Her Father's Daughter*. The theme is white supremacy, and here the attack is upon Japanese-Americans. One entire subplot recounts the struggle between all-American Donald Whiting and Oka Sayye for top position in their high school class. To achieve this end, Sayye twice attempts to murder Whiting (pp. 263, 437) and is himself murdered by one of Whiting's partisans (441-442). The latter crime is considered by characters and author alike to be wholly justified, but the theme's effect upon contemporary readers destroys their appreciation of the book. Here is Stratton-Porter's most unsound and dangerous use of sensational crime tales.

III

In addition to the crime tales, Stratton-Porter also employs mini-mysteries to enhance her stories, and one of these is both charming and funny. A major character in *The Keeper of the Bees* is a forthright, active, bright child endowed with leadership and talent. This child, the little Scout, early befriends Jamie MacFarlane and is even instrumental in thwarting a crime when the Scout and the Scout's troop drive off an imposter seeking to defraud Jamie and the Scout of a joint inheritance (pp. 375-414). But the crime tale is far less important than the mystery here, for the mystery is sustained, and not until late in the book does the reader discover whether the little Scout is a boy or a girl, despite Jamie's frequent questions and speculations.[4] This mini-mystery not only provides a subplot but also lends humor to a book badly flawed by reliance on coincidence.

The unreality of the book's main plot, Jamie's return to health and happiness, is the result of Stratton-Porter's ill-considered second mystery. When Jamie believes himself to be dying of his war wound, he agrees to marry an attractive young woman who is a total stranger. Believing her to be expecting an illegitimate child, Jamie offers the child a name to assuage her heartbreak (pp. 125-44). He then spends a major portion of the novel dreaming of the girl (who vanishes), wondering about the father of the child, and--as he recovers--speculating about the effects of his survival on the life of his bride who, of course, has every reason to suppose that she will promptly be widowed. The reader is asked to believe in this hasty marriage and in the immediate disappearance of the bride--but for her secret sorties into Jamie's home to leave bouquets as tokens of her gratitude (p. 318) or footprints as clues to her identity (pp. 229-230).

The mystery occupies Jamie throughout the novel; it perhaps served Stratton-Porter's sense of the romantic, and certainly it provides a startling frame for the nature lessons with which *The Keeper of the Bees* is rife. But it outrages the contemporary reader's ability to suspend disbelief and ultimately destroys the book.

More effective, however, are a set of mini-mysteries which share a common factor and which appear in *Freckles, A Girl of the Limberlost, Laddie, Her Father's Daughter,* and *The White Flag*. In each of these novels, some family secret not quite burried in the past haunts a major character and provokes him to speculation about his heritage. No plot can be resolved until these mysteries are solved.

For Linda Strong, of course, the mystery is not crippling. When she discovers that she has never known her true mother, she merely confirms her long-term suspicions that she and Eileen are not sisters (*Daughter*, pp. 314-315). Nor is Elnora Comstock, *A Girl of the Limberlost*, much damaged by the mystery which surrounds her father's death, except that her mother's wrongful idolization of Comstock estranges her from her daughter. But that difficulty is resolved fairly early in the novel (pp. 161-162), and Elnora is clearly marked as a survivor long before that resolution.

The mini-mystery lies closer to the center of *Laddie*. Our love story is shadowed and another threatened with destruction by a mystery buried in the past of the Pryor-Paget family whose children seek to marry into the Stanton clan. The Pryor-Paget heir has been framed for a crime he did not commit, and he must clear himself in order to be reunited with his family and to be worthy to marry Shelley Stanton. The mystery offers plot complications and opportunities for characterization, but it is resolved off-stage (pp. 566-570), and the report of the resolution, while interesting, is neither gripping nor wholly persuasive--too much depends upon coincidence and good luck.

In *Freckles* and *The White Flag*, however, despite Stratton-Porter's usual reliance upon coincidence, a child's tortured search for a parent contributes heavily to the impact of the novels. In *The White Flag*, in fact, this mini-mystery is the only redeeming quality of a novel brimming with sensationalism and heavy-handed moralizing.

Jason Peters has been reared by Marcia Peters under conditions of extreme poverty. Though Jason considers Marcia to be his mother, he is puzzled by their strangely cold relationship (p. 115) and sensitive to the fact that she has never allowed him to call her "MOther" (p. 118). Though the fact is unknown to both Jason and the community, Marcia is the mistress of wealthy, corrupt Martin Moreland, and, under pressure from him, she is eventually forced to abandon Jason and flee the town (p. 141).

Left to make his own way, Jason does so with great success, of course, but he continues to worry and to speculate about her unfeeling behavior. Eventually, he concludes that she cannot be his mother (p. 302), and he yearns to discover the secret of his parentage. In one of Stratton-Porter's most spectacularly melodramatic dénouments, it is revealed that Jason is the legitimate product of a secret marriage of Martin Moreland's youth, and the boy is briefly reunited with his real mother (pp. 431-437). The sole realistic element in this novel is Stratton-Porter's touching treatment of Jason's suffering over his sense of alienation and loss. The portrait of a child forced to believe himself an outsider not only in his community but also in his home is effective.

Freckles is a testament to the power of heredity, a factor Stratton-Porter sometimes stressed even more than environment. In this novel, the hero grows up in an institution, having been left, a battered and maimed infant, on its doorstep. Throughout his early life, the boy seeks to prove himself of worthy character, and through his job as guard of the Limberlost, he does so. Indeed, he distinguishes himself to the point that McLean, the "Boss" of the timber crew which employs Freckles, adopts the lad and makes him his heir.

Gratifying as that development is, however, Freckles is still haunted by worry that he might have been illegitimate and horrified by the supposition that his mother might have been vicious and cruel. This motif is introduced almost at once.

> Does it seem to you that anyone would take a newborn baby and row over it, until it was bruised black, cut off its hand, and leave it out on a bitter night on the steps of a charity home, to the care of strangers? That's what somebody did to me. (p. 7)

Neither his hard won proof of decency nor McLean's willingness to share name and family can banish the boy's fears, and eventually, severely injured in a lumbering accident, Freckles resigns himself to die. Though the Swamp Angel, the girl of all girls, loves him and wishes to marry him, Freckles believes his background bars him from the right to woo and win her, and he is really dying of grief over his supposed parentage.

> Can't you see that if you were willing and your father would come and offer you to me, I couldn't be touching the soles of your feet in love—me, whose people brawled over me, cut off me hand and throwed me away to freeze and to die! Me, who has no name and just as much because I've no *right* to any, as because I don't know it. When I was little, I planned to find me father and mother when I grew up. Now I know me mother deserted me, and me father was maybe a thief and surely a liar. (p. 203)

Here, too, Stratton-Porter does a good job or portraying a child's sense of loss and his need for identity. Freckles' achievements cannot assuage the boy's terror about his antecedents.

Naturally, however, this love story must "come out right" in order to fulfill the Stratton-Porter formula, so the Angel sets out to find Freckles' real family. Coincidences lead her to discover quickly and handily that Freckles' early injuries are not the result of parental abuse but wounds suffered during a fire in which his parents died trying to save him. Furthermore, he is the offspring of Irish nobility! (pp. 219-221) The mini-mystery is solved in the last pages of the novel; its solution provides the last fillip to the love story, and Stratton-Porter's belief in the importance of good family background in emphasized in this, her best novel.

IV

An examination of the seven novels under discussion here clearly reveals the dynamics of the Stratton-Porter formula which combines nature lore, love stories, and sensationalism. In every instance, some of the author's most overt exploitation of sensationalism lies in her treatment of crime stories and mini-mysteries, ingredients which she used to lend excitement to the plots. In her own way a keen student of human nature, Stratton-Porter well understood how the formula would appeal to readers, just as she understood that human beings are far from perfect creatures. Unwilling to allow for flaws in her protagonists and in other characters designed as role models for her young readers, the author reserved error for her villains, painting them in the blackest hues, and highlighting those dark tones with her crime tales. The heroes, on the other hand, are often haunted by potentially heartbreaking mini-mysteries. The solutions of these mysteries underscore the heroes' nobility and lend pathos to the books.

However, Stratton-Porter's dependence upon coincidence re-enforces the plots' sensationalism and undercuts the viability of her characters. The protagonists are meant to be strong men and women whose determination and ability make them the captains of their fates, but the impact of chance, heavily employed in every story, actually limits the characters' control over their destinies. This conflict between fate and self-determination is, like the crime tales and the mini-mysteries, never honestly confronted nor properly resolved.

For many contemporary readers, the overall effect is neither enticing nor uplifting, but the formula was, nevertheless profitable. By the time of Stratton-Porter's death, over 10,000,000 copies of her books had been sold, and the novels had been translated into at least sever foreign languages.[5] Unfortunately, the author's inability to control her flair for the sensational and her willingness to go to any length to make a moral "palatable" result in books now remembered primarily for their melodrama.

Just as Stratton-Porter's works reveal her good eye for the details of nature and a profound appreciation for natural beauty, they also demonstrate her equally keen grasp of some exciting elements of mystery and detective stories. Sadly, however, she allowed the pragmatism of the market place and a penchant for sensationalism to override both. The result is exciting plot ideas and intriguing characters mired in moralistic thrillers which exploit many plot devices of mystery-detective fiction. These devices fall far short of their potential because of the absence of genuine detection or properly controlled suspense, factors which are necessary to well wrought mystery fiction. Thus, the Stratton-Porter canon hovers between the two stools of popular romance and genuine mystery tale.

NOTES

[1] Jeanette Porter Meehan, *The Lady of the Limberlost* (Garden City, New York: Doubleday Doran & Company, Inc., 1928), pp. 305-306.

[2] S.F.E. (Eugene Francis Saxton), *Gene Stratton-Porter: A Little Story of the Life and Work and Ideals of "The Bird Woman"* (Garden City, New York: Doubleday, Page & Company, 1915), p. 39. Both the Saxton book (commissioned by Stratton-Porter's publishers) and the Meehan volume (written by Stratton-Porter's daughter) provide biased and wholly positive evaluations of the author's work. Other critics are less tolerant of the values Stratton-Porter urges. See Hazel Sample, *Pitfalls for Readers of Fiction*, Pamphlet Publication of the National Council of Teachers of English, No. 1 (Chicago, 1939-40), pp. 6-27; and Jane S. Bakerman, "Gene Stratton-Porter: What Price the Limberlost?" *The Old Northwest*, 3:2 (June 1977), 173-184.

[3] Today, Stratton-Porter is known as a writer of fiction for juveniles. *Michael O'Halloran*, *The White Flag*, and *The Keeper of the Bees* are often considered to be books for adults. It is clear, however, that the books' positive portraits of children and adolescents are intended as models for her youthful fans, an audience well established before the appearance of these volumes. Hence, the three novels are included here.

[4] The little Scout is also Stratton-Porter's interesting brief for non-sexist training for girls.

[5] Saxton, p. 47.

THE LEN DEIGHTON SERIES
By Jeff Banks and Harry D. Dawson

In the early 1960's Len Deighton rose to the top rank among writers of espionage fiction with a series of books focusing on the exploits of an anonymous operative in a super-secret British intelligence agency known to the reader only as W.O.O.C.(P.). The popularity of Deighton's spy thrillers soared after three of them, *The Ipcress File* (1962), *Funeral in Berlin* (1964), and *Billion-Dollar Brain* (1966), were made into successful movies starring Michael Caine as Deighton's secret agent. (For the movies he was given the name Harry Palmer along with a background as a petty criminal.) Deighton has continued the series, so that it now totals eight novels of varying degrees of excellence.

Among Deighton's virtues as a spy novelist is the richness of his characterizations. His hero, for instance, is a rebellious, working-class intellectual from a red-brick university who distrusts all authority and routinely ignores established procedure in his work. He is fond of good food, classical music, and women--particularly his secretary, the beautiful and efficient Jean. Capable of violence when it is warranted but determined to avoid it when it is not, he has no intention of sacrificing himself for any cause or institution.

In spite of his anti-establishment attitudes, however, Deighton's spy exhibits a grudging respect and fondness for Dawlish, the waspish spy master who, like the stereotype of his breed, is an accomplished bureaucratic intriguer with an essentially amoral attitude toward his work. Though Dawlish rules his agency with the discipline of a none-too-benevolent despot, he tolerates the unorthodox methods of his top agent because they get results. In the best tradition of British eccentricity, Dawlish cultivates in his garden not roses, but weeds, a hobby that perhaps provides an ironic commentary on the relationship of spy master and agent.

Deighton's minor characters are no less fascinating. Colonel Stok of *Funeral in Berlin* is a high-ranking KGB officer who, while stationed in East Berlin, watches Western television and buys smuggled consumer goods on the black market. He is, nonetheless, a dedicated Communist with credentials dating from the storming of the Winter Palace in 1917. Shrewd and professional, he is a match for Deighton's hero, and the two respect each other completely.

Though both *The Ipcress File* and *Funeral in Berlin* have become classics of the espionage genre, the later books in the series have been curiously uneven. This characteristic is in part a result of Deighton's attempt to bridge the gap between the realistic school of spy fiction such as that written by John le Carré and the romantic school exemplified by Ian Fleming's James Bond series. Deighton's spy is essentially an anti-hero of the type made familiar by le Carré, but occasionally he is pitted against an incredible villain such as the insane Texas millionaire, General Midwinter of *Billion-Dollar Brain*, who plots to attack the Soviet Union with a private army. In *Yesterday's Spy* (1975) Deighton's hero, in a similarly romantic vein, foils an Arab plot to bomb Israel with a nuclear device to be dropped from a giant blimp. Presumably Deighton hopes to please fans of both types of spy fiction, but the mixture doesn't jell.

Deighton's later books have been increasingly dominated by

Americans working for the CIA in a close relationship with British intelligence. This change probably reflects what is really happening in the world of international espionage as impoverished British intelligence agencies become ever more dependent upon CIA money and CIA cooperation. Unfortunately, it also tends to weaken Deighton's fiction since his American characters tend to be stereotypes or parodies of characters from the hard-boiled school of American detective and spy fiction. As such characters take over center-stage from Deighton's far more fully developed British characters, his novels become less interesting.

In spite of such shortcomings, Deighton remains one of our best spy novelists, and while the Deighton of recent years may not be the equal of the Deighton who wrote *Funeral in Berlin*, he is the equal of almost anyone else in the field. For this all his readers have reason to be grateful.

TITLE & DATE	PLACES	COMPETITION	THE PRIZE	HERO'S HELPERS
The Ipcress File 1962 (1st U.S. pb edn. 1965)	London and Great Britain --Rome--Lebanon--an obscure Pacific atoll	"Fatso", Hungary; Skip Henderson & Barney Barnes, CIA; Dalby & Jay, KGB	A brain-washed circle of fortunately placed folk privy to most British secrets	Chico Oakes,* Keightley *may have inspired Boysie Oakes series
Horse Under Water 1963 (1st U.S. edn. 1967)	Marrakech-- London and Great Britain --Portugal-- Gibraltar-- Spain	Harry Kondit independent narcotics processor; Jorge Fernandes Tomas* & Senhor Manuel de Cunha*; Charlotte Lucas-Montfort, U.S. Narc *aliases	A sunk German U-boat full of counterfeit money OR heroin OR the only list of WWII British collaborationists	"Tinkle" Bell, Lt. Clive Singleton, Joe MacIntosh, Austin Butterworth
Funeral in Berlin 1964 (1st U.S. edn. 1968)	London--E. & W. Berlin-- Bordeaux-- Czechoslovakia	Johnnie Vulkan, independent operator; Samantha Steel, Shin Bet; Col. Stok, KGB	A top E. German scientist OR a Nazi war criminal OR a fabulous cache of WWII treasure	Chico, Ossie Butterworth, Keightley
The Billion Dollar Brain 1966 (1st U.S. edn. 1966	London-- Finland-- NYC-- Texas-- Russia	Harvey Newbegin, Gen. Midwinter's private spy agency; Col. Stok, KGB; Ross, British Foreign Office	A smuggled, deadly virus AND/OR provocation of WWIII	Chico, Lt. Col. Harriman
An Expensive Place to Die 1966 (1st U.S. pb edn. 1968)	Paris and rural France	Hudson, U.S.; M. Datt & Jean Paul Pascal, France (partly); Kuang-t'ien, Red China	A double handle on the West: sex orgy blackmail of VIPs & H-Bomb blackmail	None, but Martin L. Byrd is his case officer
Spy Story 1974 (1st U.S. pb edn. 1968)	Scots and Scandinavian waters--London--Norway	Stok, KGB; Ben Toliver, independent British group; Col. Schlegel, CIA	Naval supremacy in the North Sea gained by bluff, defection	Ferdy Foxwell, more-or-less
Yesterday's Spy 1975 (1st U.S. pb edn., 1976	London-- Wales-- Switzerland-- W. Germany-- France	Steve Champion & Gus Aziz, U.A.R.; Claude Winkler, Gehlen Bureau	An A-Bomb for the Arabs, with a weird but credible delivery system	None, but Schlegel is now case officer
Catch a Falling Spy 1976 U.S. pb ed. 1977	Sahara, Paris rural France, Ireland, U.S. East Coast	Gerry Hart, Douglas Reid-Kennedy, Mrs. K. Bekuv, all KGB	The ultimate in electronic snooping, leading to world supremacy	None; he works directly for Maj. Mickey Mann

HIGHLIGHTS	REMARKS
Chap. 4 reminds (deliberately) of *1984*--hero-narrator's choice of language, especially in summing up the "pickles" he is in at chap. endings--hero bearing up under prolonged interrogation & brain-washing--rather Bondish escape.	Dedicated to man who inspired Cavendish--"appendix" is really Notes, building verisimilitude--astrological readings for chap. headquotations--headquotations for whole book from Shakespeare (*Henry IV*) & Gilbert White--B.J.D. (perhaps Harry) Harrison, hero's alias--good analogical history of the Atomic Age in chap. 18.
Hero's service skindiving course--literal exploding of Mac--tapping famous phone-tapper's phone--Italian diver's anecdotes approaching Garvin in the Modesty Blaise books--stowing away on villain's boat--fight with Fernie--brilliant dialogic suggestion of foreign accent in chap. 53--hero's final escape from da Cunha.	Headquotations for book by Sir Walter Scott & Callingham on seamanship--book purports to be a confidential report--6 "authenticating" appendices--debate on "ethics" of spying--chap. 38 borrows a Spillane gimmick--probably more chaps. (59) than in any other significant spy book--one of the gimmicks da Cunha is working on is reverse of Vonnegut's main sci fi device in *Cat's Cradle*.
Introduction of recurring KGB officer--continued, intermittent verbal duel between hero and Dawlish--flashback chaps. in WWII--serendipitous uncovering of a British neo-Nazi--death of Vulkan--the Guy Fawkes Night showdown with final baddie.	Book headquotations: news report of conversation between Allen Dulles & Kruschev + Southey, Einstein & R. Lewishon--most chap. headquotations are elementary chess instructions--chap. titles are dates, showing book covers 37 days in 1963--hero's cover name is Edmond Dorf--five "authenticating" appendices.
Hero's capture by KGB--a right-wingers' masquerade party--driving over ocean ice in a Volkswagon--.atvian truck hi-jacking--movie-style gunslinger tricks--discovery of dentist's victim--forcing confession from Dr. Pike--failed attempt to kidnap Newbegin from train--a few interesting satiric shots at James Bond.	Book headquotations: a Russian proverb, J. Paul Getty, the Kalevala--nursery rhyme headquotations for the 10 sections--hero's cover name, Liam Dempsey, is a tip of the hat to le Carre's *The Spy Who Came in from the Cold*, as are the multiple false defections--most of the U.S. part of the book seems a response to Spillane's Tiger Mann series--author's first venture into nostalgia.
Hero's fight with five foes at once--LSD victimization of hero--public and covert reactions to the first death in chapters 14 & 15--barroom brawl--hi-jacking the blackmail dossiers.	Trevanian's *The Loo Sanction* is cognate book--headquotations: O. Wilde, Mohammed & instructions for the Elysee Palace Guards--almost 1/3 chaps. are from female p.o.v. & several are in 3rd Person--hero's cover is T. Davis, artist--no Dawlish.
Hero's rough & tumble with a pair of Stok's toughs--a party with the landed gentry--escape from Toliver's base (a real cliffhanger)--playing tag under the ice with Red subs--a Stok doublecross--a trek over the ice.	Condon's *Arigato*, though not a spy novel, is an important partial cognate--book headquotations by Cowper--chap. headquotations on gamesmanship--hero's cover is as Pat Armstrong, working for NATO War Games Studies Center--Dawlish is an infrequently appearing *deus ex machina*.
WWII flashbacks remind of *Funeral*--expert "toss" of rooms--nice, continuous sparing between old pros--hero's arrest by French police--chap. 18 explanation of Theory of Relativity--motorcyclists machinegun a limosine.	THE nostalgic spy novel (Garfield's *Hop-Scotch*, Hamilton's *The Terminators*, O'Brine's *No Earth for Foxes* & Harris's *Black Sunday* are all partial cognates)--hero uses WWII cover name of Charlie Bonnard--all the literary-scholarly paraphernalia has been wisely dropped.
Mugging attempt following a posh party--knife attack after church--verbal sparring--rocket attack at end--endless action, more intellection than in other books.	Headquotation is "epitaph of an astronomer"--hero's cover is Frederick L. Anthony, tourist-banker & he is temporarily seconded to the U.S.--full of Spillane parody, some of it brilliant.

KIM PHILBY, MASTER SPY
IN FACT AND FICTION

By Theodore P. Dukeshire

Born to an upper-class British family, Harold Adrian Russell Philby--known to his friends as "Kim"--attended Westminster School and Cambridge University and seemed, outwardly at least, to be a solid member of the British Establishment.

After graduation from Cambridge Philby became a journalist, covering Franco's side of the Spanish Civil War for *The Times*. During World War II he served in British counterintelligence, and by the war's end Philby headed the entire counterintelligence operation.

His position as First Secretary in charge of liaison with the United States on security matters sent Philby to Washington in 1949. When his friends Guy Burgess and Donald MacLean defected to Russia in 1951 Philby was sent back to Britain and fired. He lived in obscurity until the British government sent him to the Middle East to work as a journalist.

On a January night in 1955 Philby, either sensing the government was on to him or for some other reason, disappeared from Beirut, only to emerge in Moscow where he is still living.

After Philby's defection a spate of books came out chronicling his life and activities. Among the best are *The Philby Conspiracy* by *Times* writers Bruce Page, David Lietch and Phillip Knightly, with a foreword by John LeCarre (British title: *Philby: The Spy Who Betrayed a Generation*); *The Third Man* by E. H. Cookridge; and Philby's *My Silent War*, with a foreword by Graham Greene.

In his foreword to *The Philby Conspiracy* John LeCarre asks, Is there a fourth man still in British intelligence? Who originally recruited Philby, Burgess and MacLean? Who controlled them during their active years? Chris Scott uses these questions as background for his novel, *To Catch a Spy*. In this book, a fourth man, George Michael Stevens, has defected to Moscow, and nine months later is reported dead of a heart attack. British journalist Bill Johnson goes to Moscow to find out the truth about Stevens. Was he a Soviet agent? Or was he a double, so trusted by the KGB that he could ferret out information or carry out a mission? As Johnson progresses he runs across the "old boy" network that includes "Carlo" Peat, who had originally recruited Stevens, and Sir Donald MacPherson of British intelligence.

Alan Williams' *Gentleman Traitor* is a "What If" book which asks what would happen if Philby wanted to defect back to Britain.

Philby's life in Beirut and Moscow is chronicled by his wife Eleanor in *Kim Philby: The Spy I Married*. It's a gossipy book about Philby and Burgess and MacLean. She thought MacLean a pompous ass and couldn't stand MacLean's wife Melinda for "stealing" Kim from her. MacLean also wouldn't allow Purdy and Sutherland's book, *Burgess and MacLean,* in his home because it depicted MacLean as a homosexual.

While these books are but a smattering of books on Philby and spying, they do present a rounded picture of the outward man. But no account of reading can answer the question, What makes a man turn against the things that should mean the most to his life.

BOUCHERCON, 1978: IX AND COUNTING

By Donald A. Yates

Each year since it was first convened in May of 1970 to honor the memory of the late Anthony Boucher, the Bouchercon has built its attendance figures steadily up to and past one hundred and then on toward two hundred registered fans. The ninth version of this appealing mystery lover's smorgasbord, held October 6-8, 1978, at Chicago's Bismarck Hotel, attracted a goodly number of participants--comfortably within expectations--and I, for one, am grateful that this event can still be carried out in an atmosphere of relaxed intimacy. Indeed, there may not be more than two hundred hard-core mystery fans to be convened anywhere at any one time--outside New York City--and, in any case, ever larger numbers are clearly not necessary to assure success.

I know that Otto Penzler and Chris Steinbunner's Bouchercon VIII in Gotham last year was a splendid success--on a large scale--and I am genuinely sorry to have missed it. Yet the ninth Bouchercon in Chicago seemed to me to produce the special small-scale pleasures that few such gatherings can so consistently provide. And you always meet such interesting people....

I drove over to Chicago early on Friday with Carry J. Black, the Detroit mystery collector and connoisseur. Chicago *does* still have good second-hand bookstores, if you know where to find them. Cary knew of some North Side places I hadn't been to, and I introduced him to the North Clark Street string of bookshops. By the time the registration desk opened at the Bismarck early Friday evening, Cary and I had already made the rounds. (And a rewarding reconnaisance it was.)

The first activity in the hotel's lower-level meeting rooms centered around the displays of three book dealers who enhanced the proceedings by exhibiting first-rate selections of mystery magaxines, hardcovers and paperbacks. The three were Robert Weinberg of Chicago, Mary Ann Grochowski, who operates Suspense Unlimited of South Milwaukee, and Ray Walsh of East Lansing's Curious Bookshop, all of whom appeared to do a brisk business over the two-day period.

In these propitiously bookish surroundings, fans, participants, and organizers began to gather. The local hosts--Bob hahn, John Nieminski, and Ely Liebow--had no trouble making all feel welcome. And the generous warmth and good-will of Mystery Writers of America president Robert L. Fish and his wife Mame established a genuinely cordial mood.

After a hurried dinner on the town, fans made their way back to the Bismarck for a mystery film program. An ancient silent movie version of a Nick Carter exploit preceded the feature film, *The Curse of the Living Corpse*, which appeared to be a good choice to satisfy the audience's opening-night appetite for sensation. However, as the evening wore on, night spots and upstairs parties (in the best tradition) lured away some of the audience.

Saturday morning dawned cool and fair. The book displays opened up for the early birds and by mid-morning the formal program of panels and speakers was underway. There were about a dozen separate sessions spaced over the two-day span, almost equally divided between individual talks and panel discussions-- in all, a nice mixture of topics and opinions. To start things rolling, Bob Briney reminisced, under the rubric of "Murder Behind Locked Doors", about the late Anthony Boucher, the detective fiction critic, author and historian whose contributions he had helped to acknowledge by establishing the Bouchercon nearly a decade ago.

His remarks were followed by a panel of speakers who offered appreciations of three Chicago writers. Mike Nevins, who is unmatched on the subject, evoked once again the image of the wild and wooly genius of mystery fiction, Harry Stephen Keeler, whose widow Thelma faithfully attended all the sessions. Mary Ann Grochowski gave a sympathetic and well-researched evaluation of Craig Rice, who worked out of Chicago before heading to the West Coast in 1946. Finally, Bob Hahn strung together some fond recollections of his friendship with the late, beloved author, Sherlockian and bookman, Vincent Starrett.

In the first afternoon session, Robert L. Fish, Chris Steinbrunner and Ely Liebow together came down pretty hard on the recent spate of apocryphal books dealing with doings around Baker Street. Few titles got as much as grudging praise and one in particular (Michael Dibdin's *The Last Sherlock Holmes Story*) was roundly denounced as an abomination. (I myself had reached the judgement that it was structurally flawed and fascinatingly repulsive.)

John J. McAleer, biographer of Rex Stout, next gave a colorful profile of his subject, dropping here and there anecdotes that through discretion had not found their way into his biography of Stout, a heafty and valuable volume published and already in its third printing in 1977. The special insights that a scholar such as McAleer can offer into a celebrated mystery author are the sort of thing that make these gatherings truly memorable.

Next, I took the floor to talk about the contributions of Agatha Christie. With barely three days notice, I put together some remarks that tried to

BOB BRINEY

MIKE NEVINS AND
MARY ANN GROCHOWSKI

BOB HAHN

BOB FISH, ELY LIEBOW & CHRIS STEINBRUNNER

JOHN MCALEER

DON YATES

suggest something of the life and achievements of the "High Ppiestess of Mystification". (of the two panelists originally scheduled to speak on this subject, one had developed influenza and the other stage fright.)

To cap off the afternoon session, Jane S. Bakerman, J. Randolph Cox, and Robert Eckels gave their impressions of a number of new (or relatively new: Ruth Rendell and P.D. James) mystery writers who, in their opinion, deserved watching.

COX, BAKERMAN AND ECKELS

Adjournment until the pre-banquet cocktail party was the signal for new friends and old to slip off to convenient watering spots or private rooms upstairs to carry on enthusiastic discussions of authors, books, ideas, shoptalk and just plain gossip. The evening festivities were graced with the presence of Phyllis White, widow of Anthony Boucher, and the principal guest speaker, Walter B. Gibson (a.k.a. Maxwell Grant), whom fate had singled out to present to an unsuspecting world the immortal figure of The Shadow.

After dinner was cleared away, Phyllis White expressed her appreciation for the homage that was fondly rendered by friends and admirers of her late husband. Then the rowdy and (necessarily) drunken high-ranking officers of Hugo's Companions, the Chicago Sherlockian scion society, took over the spotlight to perpetrate a series of arcane rites and ceremonies. In some mysterious manner, the Companions were holding one of their monthly meetings simultaneously with the banquet proceedings, and those present will recall that two worthy Chicago Sherlockians were taken into the scion's bosom and were presented with handsome documents attesting to their new status.

WALTER B. GIBSON

As the main banquet speaker, Walter B. Gibson won the sympathies and admiration of his listeners with his good-natured, anecdote-filled remarks on his experiences as The Shadow's progenitor. As a surprise added attraction, Gibson concluded by entertaining his audience with a series of magic tricks, which he carried off with the witty, disarming style of the accomplished prestidigitator.

Soon after the banquet ended, a movie screen was set up and for the fans with an appetite for still more entertainment, a late-night bill of films began to reel off. The first of these was an installment of an early serial featuring Victor Jory as The Shadow. It turned out to be an unintentionally hilarious episode that seemed--at this distance in time--riddled with clichés and impossibly wooden dialog. Hard-core film addicts were then treated to *23 Paces to Baker Street*. Before very many paces were measured off, the late-night parties began to claim willing revelers.

It may seem to the reader of these remarks that I stress too much the non-official features of the Bouchercon. But since attendance is still in the modest range, just about anyone who wants to sit in on some lively conversation with a favorite mystery author, or critic, or bookseller, or publisher can find an upstairs room where he is welcomed and where such conversations are going on--far into the night. This is yet another benefit of these gatherings. To such an after-dinner informal party I owe my friendship with the late Cornell Woolrich, whom I met at a private party following the 1960 MWA Awards Dinner at the Astor Hotel in New York City. I'll always be grateful.

The events of Sunday morning were late and a bit ragged in getting started. Since scheduled speaker Stuart Kaminsky did not put in an appearance, the sessions were juggled around somewhat and the mid-morning program began with a quickly-assembled panel comprised of editors of "fanzines". This was perhaps the most lively and unusual feature of Bouchercon IX. Consider the prospect of the following authorities gathered at one table to discuss the nature and importance of the relatively new phenom-

SCOTT, MEYERSON, NIEMINSKI, BRINEY, TOWNSEND, LIEBOW

enon of the small-circulation magazine edited for the mystery fan: Art Scott of DAPA-EM (as specialized as a newsletter can get); Jeff Meyerson of *The Poisoned Pen*; John Nieminski, co-editor of *Baker Street Miscellanea*; Bob Briney of *The Rohmer Review*; Guy Townsend, the moving force behind *The MYSTERY FANcier*; and Otto Penzler, who has generously taken over from Publisher's Inc. of Del Mar, California, the publication of the granddaddy of them all, *The Armchair Detective*, which was on the verge of slipping into the consequence of insolvency--oblivion. (Bless you, Otto, and your Mysterious Press!") [*Otto had not arrived at the time the above photo was taken, and Ely was chairing the discussion.*]

This panel's comments were insightful and illuminating, and the audience joined in enthusiastically in the free-wheeling discussion that ensued. The morning segment was concluded with Warren Scheideman's interesting illustrated chat entitled "A Fine Set of Portraits", in which he made some unusual deductions about the varying talents of the several artists who illustrated the Sherlock Holmes tales as they appeared in the *Strand Magazine*.

The afternoon program was brief but extremely informative and entertaining. Robert Weinberg gave an illustrated talk on "The Shadow and Company", in which he reviewed some of the early pulp magazine characters and treated us to a dazzling slide show of pulp cover art of half a century ago. He was followed by Chuck Schaden, who presented an eminently literate and delightful evocation of old-time radio shows, organized under the title "Those Were the Days . . . and Nights." The convention thus closed on a high note.

CHUCK SCHADEN

The next Bouchercon is tentatively scheduled for Los Angeles in 1979. And there seems to be absolute assurance that Bouchercon XI will be held in 1980 in Washington, D.C., "Where [as the program announcement suggests] Crime Is Your Government's Business."

Cary Black and I motored back

to Michigan in a state of idle bliss, sorting through our fresh impressions and recollections. We felt it all had been a great success.

. . .

Postscript: Four days later, the last piece fell into place. At the banquet dinner a table companion of mine had been Russell Atwood, a very bright young fellow in his mid-teens who had come from Massachusetts with his father to attend the Bouchercon. He knew an awesome amount of things about detective fiction--authors, titles, dates, plots, and assorted exotic lore. I was impressed. Straying a bit afield, I found an area in which his knowledge was slightly imperfect. He couldn't recall the names of the three actors who played Dorothy's three over-the-rainbow companions in *The Wizard of Oz*. I confidently identified all three. Then young Russell said, "Do you know what their names were in the Kansas farm black-and-white segment of the movie?" I was stumped, not to say stunned. "Think about it," he suggested not unkindly, as I suddenly noted that the person on my right was trying to get my attention. Four days after I returned from Chicago, the letter came in the mail. It contained a single business card: Atwood Security Serviece, Inc., Special Services, Mass.--Conn. Master Atwood's name was typed on the front. On the back of the card: "Dear Mr. Yates; the names are:
    Hunk--The Scarecrow--Ray Bolger
    Hickory--The Tin Woodsman--Jack Haley
    Zeke--The Cowardly Lion--Bert Lahr
                   Thanks from the
                   A.B.M.C. '78
                   teenager."
You do meet such interesting people.

THE NERO WOLFE SAGA
PART XI
By Guy M. Townsend

"Easter Parade" [Easter, 1956], published in *And Four to Go*, 1958.
    THE STORY ::: Wolfe--"Mr. Millard Bynoe has produced a flamingo-pink Vanda--both petals and sepals true pink, with no tints, spots, or edgings. . . . But I don't believe it. I have it from Mr. Lewis Hewitt, who had it from Mr. Bynoe's gardener, but I don't believe it. As you know, I have been hybridizing for a pink Vanda for years, and have come no closer to it than the rose-lilac of peetersiana or the magenta of sandarae. I don't believe it, and I have to see it." Bynoe having declined to conform its existence over the phone, and having neglected to invite Wolfe to drop by for a peek, Wolfe's orchidmania leads him to concoct a wild scheme to get his hands on some blossoms from the plant. Rumor has it that Mrs. Bynoe will be wearing a spray of the flowers on Easter Sunday, and Wolfe has Archie hire someone to snatch the spray from her bosom as she leaves church. Archie is to be in attendance with color film in the Centrex camera as a back-up should the snatch fail to come off. Wolfe gets the spray all right, but Mrs. Bynoe dies immediately afterwards from a strychnine-loaded needle in the abdomen, and it looks as though Wolfe is going to have to own up to being an accomplice to larceny before he pulls it out by a piece of fantastic good luck. Wolfe's dignity and his detectival prowess are not at their highest polish in this one, but it's an entertaining tale for all that.
    WOLFE ::: Wolfe's desire for the pink orchid is overwhelming--"I would give three thousand dollars for that plant"--but it lands him in such a position of potential trouble that he later makes the incredible statement, "I wish I had never heard of orchids." This is, however, merely a temporary aberration. Archie tells us, at story's end, "If you would like to see the plant of flamingo-pink Vanda, ring me and if I'm not too busy I'll arrange it. It has a spot all to itself on a bench up in the plant rooms. It came in addition to Bynoe's check in payment of Wolfe's bill for services rendered. I have no proof that Wolfe dropped any hints to Bynoe about the Vanda, but I wasn't with him when he visited Bynoe's greenhouses, and I am entitled to my opinion." Wolfe says, "There are only four people of whom I would ask a favor," and one of them is Archie. Wolfe's weight is one-seventh of a ton. Cramer calls him "just a big gob of egomania."
    ARCHIE ::: Archie uses his notebook. He speaks of his height--"my own six feet"--and remarks that "while I can no longer do the hundred in 10:7, I can move."
    OTHER REGULARS ::: Fred and Orrie are just mentioned, and Archie talks to Lon on the phone. Fritz, of course, is around --Wolfe says "my cook is unsurpassed, if not unequaled." D.A. Skinner [he was Commissioner Skinner in the previous episode-- how many times have I screwed this up?] is present. And Cramer is too--"His keen blue-gray eyes, looking smaller than they were on account of his big round face." Rowcliff gets mentioned: Cramer asks, "How would you like to come downtown for a session with Lieutenant Rowcliff?" to which Archie replies, "I'd love it. I once got him stuttering in eight minutes, the

best I ever did, and I'd like--".

PHYSICAL ASPECTS ::: Archie gives the address as 918 West Thirty-fifth Street. There are still seven steps in the front stoop, and inside the front door is "the big old oak rack", which, we learn, has a shelf for hats and individual hangers for coats, and stands across the hall from the front room. The door between the office and the front room is still sound-proofed. Inside the office the red leather chair is located "near the end of Wolfe's desk." There is a swinging door into the kitchen (from the hall), and in the kitchen are "two refrigerators, one cool and one cold", "a long table in the center", and "my breakfast table against the wall". Archie goes "to the basement to shoot pool", and he gets "the sedan from the garage". The second and third floors appear to be back in their proper places in this one--Wolfe says to a man who is staying over, "There is a comfortable room on the third floor of this house."

ROUTINE AT THE BROWNSTONE ::: "It was half past six, still daylight, as I mounted the stoop of the brownstone, used my key, and found, to my surprise, that the chain-bolt wasn't on", so it must have become a regular thing again. Archie is still the doorbell answerer. Lastly, here's something we've not encountered before: "It was a pleasant scene, the egomaniac having, as usual, his Sunday-evening snack with the cook. Fritz was on a stool at the long table in the center, steering a dripping endive core to his open mouth. Wolfe, seated at my breakfast table against the wall, was pouring honey on stearing halves of buttermilk biscuits."

If Death Ever Slept [May-June 1957], published in 1957.

THE STORY ::: Of all the rules which Wolfe has established to regulate his professional and private lives, probably none is more adamantly adhered to than the one against taking domestic cases. So, when millionaire Otis Jarrell seeks to hire Wolfe to get the goods on his daughter-in-law so that his son will dovirce her, our obvious expectation is that Wolfe will turn the job down flat. Even when Jarrell adds that he wants Wolfe to prove that the daughter-in-law has been selling his business secrets to his competitors, the case still is essentially domestic, and as such untouchable for Wolfe in the normal course of things. But things are not normal at the brownstone, as Wolfe and Archie are in the midsts of a spat and each tries to outdo the other with Jarrell present, with the result that Wolfe takes the case. Later Wolfe remarks: "I will concede that we blundered into this mess by a collaboration in mulishness." And so they did. The upshot of it all is that Archie goes to the Jarrell penthouse apartment in the guise of Otis Jarrell's new secretary, intent on ferreting out proof of the dastardly daughter-in-law's perfidy. As might be expected, the case does not long remain one of mere domestic difficulties, since a few corpses turn up here and there to complicate things. It is the longest time before Wolfe can lay his hands on the murderer, but of course he does in the end. Not the best or most gripping episode in the Saga, but a fun read nonetheless.

WOLFE ::: The cause of the tiff between Wolfe and Archie is instructive as to their personalities. When Archie gets home at 2:00 a.m. and finds Wolfe still up and reading in the office, the latter crossly demands to know where Archie has been.

He was glaring. "I should have asked, where have you *not* been.

Miss Rowan has telephoned five times, first shortly after eight o'clock, last half an hour ago. If I had gone to bed she wouldn't have let me sleep. As you know, Fritz was out for the evening."

"Hasn't he come home?"

"Yes, but he must be up to get breakfast and I didn't want him pestered. You said you were going to the Flamingo Club with Miss Rowan. You didn't. She telephoned five times. So I, not you, have spent the evening with her, and I haven't enjoyed it."

Archie explains thusly: "I took the elevator up to her penthouse and found that there were people there she knows I don't like. So I beat it. Where I went is irrelevant." Archie says Wolfe's weight is nearly a hundred pounds more than Archie's own 178. Wolfe has a couple of quotables in this episode: "Murder sometimes creates only ripples, but more frequently high seas", and "You may meet importunity that will make me a model of amenity by comparison." He also says "per contra". Archie says, "I'll say one thing for Wolfe, he hates to have anyone else's meal interrupted almost as much as his own", and "Mr. Wolfe never talks business at the table." This episode is important as the first (and only?) one in which it is suggested that Wolfe actually sells his plants: Archie says Wolfe is "a practicing private detective with no other source of income except selling a few orchid plants now and then." "He usually takes three little sips of coffee at its hottest before putting the cup down." "Wolfe doesn't often bellow, and almost never at anyone but Cramer or me, but when he does he means it." "When he uses his mind he leans back and closes his eyes, and when he's hard at it his lips go in and out." There's something faintly embarrassing about this item: "When I speak to a man, or a woman, I like to look at him, but I speak now to the one who took the gun, and I can't look at him because I don't know who he is. So, speaking to him, I close my eyes." When Cramer accuses Wolfe of holding back evidence proving his client guilty, Wolfe has Archie take $3,000 from the office safe and then Wolfe waves it at Cramer: "The wager is that when this is over and the facts are known you will acknowledge that at this hour, Monday evening, I had no inkling of the identity of the murderer, except that I had surmised that it was one of the seven people I have named, and I have told you that. Three thousand dollars to three dollars. One thousand to one. You have three dollars. Mr. Stebbins can hold the stakes." Cramer doesn't take the bet. Then follows this exchange: WOLFE: "Do you believe in words of honor?" CRAMER: "I do when the honor is there." WOLFE: "Am I a man of honor?" "Cramer's eyes widened. He was flabbergasted. He started to answer and stopped. He had to consider. 'You may be at that,' he allowed. 'You're tricky, you're foxy, you're the best liar I know, but if anybody asked me to name something you had done that was dishonorable I'd have to think.'" WOLFE: "Very well, think." CRAMER: "Skip it. Say you're a man of honor. What about it?" Archie of Wolfe: "Add his opinion of women to his opinion of other detectives, and you get his opinion of women detectives."

ARCHIE ::: Archie weighs 178 pounds. He tells us again that the furniture in his bedroom is his own, and that "I have a Kirman there, paid for by me, 8'4" X 3'2"." Archie takes several drinks in this one--scotch and water. Of cigars he says, "I don't smoke them myself, but I admit that the finest tobacco smell you can get is a whiff from the lit end of a fine Havana." Of television he says, "I have no TV favorites, because most of the programs seem to be intended for either the under-brained or the over-brained and I come in between." [It is extremely difficult to believe that there ever were any TV programs intended for the over-brained.] Archie says he does not go to church. He does some dancing in this one, at Colonna's and at the Flamingo Club, and he plays bridge. And he says he walked "the thirty blocks to stretch my legs." "Whenever possible I go out every morning, some time between nine and eleven, when Wolfe is up in the plant room, to loosen my legs and get a lungfull of exhaust fumes." I think this is the first mention of that habit. Archie speaks of his "usual forty minutes with the morning *Times*". Archie says "There were four guys--one at headquarters, one on the D.A.'s staff, and two on Homicide--for whom I had done favors in the past" and who owed him favors in return. Lastly, Archie says that something "was rather unindomitable".

OTHER REGULARS ::: With Archie pretending to be "Alan Green", Jarrell's secretary, someone had to pretend to be Archie Goodwin, and Orrie Cather was elected. (The "Orrie" is short for Orville this time.) Not surprisingly, there is some friction between the two. As noted earlier, Lily Rowen is mentioned, but she does not appear. Felix at Rusterman's is mentioned, as is Theodore of the green thumb. Archie talks to Lon Cohen on the phone and goes by the *Gazette* to office to see him. "Lon is a fine guy and a good poker player." Lewis Hewitt is just mentioned, as are Assistant D.A. Mandelbaum and Police Commissioner Kelly. Rowcliff is mentioned, too: "I liked nothing better than twisting Rowcliff's ear"; "Rowcliff would be nasty to Saint Peter, if he ever got near him." Nathaniel Parker is called upon to spring Archie. Sally Colt, of Dol Bonner's agency, makes another appearance, as does Dol herself, "a very attractive sight for a female dick, with her home-grown long black lashes making a curling canopy for her caramel-colored eyes". Wolfe invites her to breakfast; Archie says "Fritz would be on needles." Fritz, Archie says, "suspects every woman who ever crosses the threshold of wanting to take over his kitchen, not to mention the rest of the house." Archie gives us a quick run-down on Saul, Fred, Orrie and Dol: "Saul's rate was sixty bucks a day and expenses and he was worth at least five times that. Fred Durkin was good but no Saul Panzer. Orrie Cather, whom you have seen at my desk, was yes and no. On some tricks he was unbeatable, but on others not so hot. As for Dol Bonner, I didn't know much about her first-hand, but the word around was that if you had to have a female dick she was it. She had her own office and staff." Then there are "two of Mr. Wolfe's oldest and dearest enemies, and mine, . . . Inspector Cramer and Sergeant Stebbins of Homicide." Archie describes Cramer as "a husky specimen in a gray suit, a pair of broad shoulders, and a big red face." "I would say that Inspector Cramer and Sergeant Stebbins weigh about the same, around one-ninety, and little or none of it is fat on either of them, so you would suppose their figures would pretty well match, but they don't. Cramer's flesh is tight-weave and Stebbins' is loose-weave. On Cramer's hands the skin follows the line of the bones, whereas on Stebbins' hands you have to take the bones for granted, and presumably they are like that all over, though I have never played with them on the beach and so can't swear to it. I'm not sure which of them would be the toughest to tangle with, but some day I may find out, even if they are officers of the law." Archie, of

Cramer's cigars: "He never lit one." Purley's antagonism for Wolfe is, as usual, barely suppressed. "Purley Stebbins' chair was where he always put it himself if we didn't, against the wall at arm's length from Cramer." When Archie replies "Fifth amendment" to one of Cramer's questions, Cramer says, "Nuts. That's for Reds and racketeers, not for clowns like you."

ROUTINE AT THE BROWNSTONE ::: Archie says he checks up beforehand "when it's feasible on everyone who makes an appointment to see Wolfe". "The phone rang. I swiveled and got it, and I noticed that Wolfe reached for his too, which he rarely does unless I give him a sign." "One of the standing rules in that house is that when we are at the table, and nothing really hot is on, Fritz answers the phone in the kitchen, and if it seems urgent I go and get it. There may be something or somebody Wolfe would leave the table for, but I don't know what or who." "During meals Fritz was supposed to get" the doorbell. We've seen this one before: after lunch "we had crossed to the office and coffee had been poured." Archie does his own minor mending--he is "sewing buttons on pajamas".

PHYSICAL ASPECTS ::: "I left the house and went across the street to the tailor shop, from where there was a good view of our stoop." "He had ten thousand orchids in his plant rooms on the roof; I had one African violet on my windowsill, and it wasn't feeling well." A newspaper rack is mentioned (I think for the first time), and it appears to be located in the kitchen. Archie mentions that Cramer "tossed his hat on the bench" in the hallway (another first, I believe). The balance of the physical aspects covered in this episode are in the office. The office safe is mentioned, as are some filing cabinets "as tall as me" (another first), the couch and the big globe. Over the phone Archie tells Wolfe to "please remind Orrie that the bottom drawer of my desk is personal and there's nothing in it he needs." The chair at Archie's desk "had cost $139.95; the one he [Wolfe] was sitting in, orvesized and custom-made of Brazilian Mauro, had come to $650.00." The paperweight on Wolfe's desk is mentioned again--"a chunk of jade that a woman had once used to crack her husband's skull." Then there's the peephole: "The hole, ten inches square, was at eye level in the wall twelve feet to the right of Wolfe's desk. On the office side it was covered by what appeared to be just a pretty picture of a waterfall. On the other side, in a wing of the hall across from the kitchen, it was covered by nothing, and you could not only see through but also hear through. My longest stretch there was one night when we had four people in the front room waiting for Wolfe to show up (he was in the kitchen chinning with Fritz) and we were expecting and hoping that one of them would sneak into the office to get something from a drawer of Wolfe's desk, and we wanted to know which one. That time I stood there at that hole more than three hours, and the door from the front room never opened." Archie says a person at the peephole has a good view of anyone at his desk as well as a client, presumably in the red chair, but that Wolfe could only be seen "in profile", and then "only by sticking my nose into the hole and pressing my forehead against the upper edge."

ODDS AND ENDS ::: There's $3,700 in the safe, plus about $200 in petty cash. Wolfe returns a retainer, but he gets paid in the end anyway.

AN INDEX OF BOOKS REVIEWED IN TMF VOLUME 2
Compiled by David H. Doerrer

Author, Title (Reviewer)	Issue:Page
Adams, Clifton, DEATH'S SWEET SONG (Steve Lewis)	2:35
Aickman, Robert, COLD HAND IN MINE (Steve Lewis)	6:31
Alexander, David, DIE, LITTLE GOOSE (Steve Lewis)	1:30
Alexander, Patrick, DEATH OF A THIN-SKINNED ANIMAL (Steve Lewis)	4:36
_____, ditto (Jane S. Bakerman)	5:35
Alverson, Charles, NOT SLEEPING, JUST DEAD (Steve Lewis)	2:34
Ambler, Eric, A COFFIN FOR DIMITRIOS (Martin Morse Wooster)	4:39
Anthony, David, STUD GAME (Myrtis Broset)	6:42
Anthony, Evelyn, THE RENDEZVOUS (Myrtis Broset)	1:39
_____, THE SILVER FALCON (Myrtis Broset)	6:42
Archer, Jeffrey, SHALL WE TELL THE PRESIDENT? (Thomas L. Motsinger)	6:36
Arrighi, Mel, TURKISH WHITE (Steve Lewis)	1:23
Ashford, Jeffrey, HOSTAGE TO DEATH (Steve Lewis)	5:26
_____, SLOW DOWN THE WORLD (Steve Lewis)	1:28
Asimov, Issac, ASIMOV'S SHERLOCKIAN LIMERICKS (Martin Morse Wooster)	4:42
Asinof, Eliot, SAY IT AIN'T SO, GORDON LITTLEFIELD (Steve Lewis)	3:45
Atkey, Bertram, MR. DASS: A NOVEL OF PURSUIT AND PUNISHMENT (Charles Shibuk)	5:37
Avallone, Michael, THE BIG STIFFS (Stephen Mertz)	5:39
Bagby, George, THE ORIGINAL CARCASE (Steve Lewis)	4:34
_____, THE TOUGH GET GOING (Steve Lewis)	6:33
Ballard, W.T., SAY YES TO MURDER (Stephen Mertz)	3:54
_____, THE SEVEN SISTERS (Stephen Mertz)	5:40
Barclay, Stephen, BLOCKBUSTER (Steve Lewis)	1:21
Bartram, George, THE AELIAN FRAGMENT (Steve Lewis)	5:31
Bernard, Trevor, BRIGHTLIGHT (R. Jeff Banks)	1:31
_____, ditto (Myrtis Broset)	1:37
_____, ditto (Steve Lewis)	4:32
Bingham, John, MINISTRY OF DEATH (Steve Lewis)	5:26
Black, Ian Stuart, THE MAN ON THE BRIDGE (Steve Lewis)	1:27
Blair, Lucinda, THE PLACE OF DEVILS (Myrtis Broset)	1:37
Block, Lawrence, BURGLARS CAN'T BE CHOOSERS (Steve Lewis)	4:36
_____, THE SINS OF THE FATHERS (Steve Lewis)	4:30
Bova, Ben, THE MULTIPLE MAN (Myrtis Broset)	1:36
Braine, John, THE PIOUS AGENT (Theodore P. Dukeshire)	3:52
Brand, Christianna, GREEN FOR DANGER (Martin Morse Wooster)	6:38
Branston, Frank, AN UP AND COMING MAN (Steve Lewis)	1:25
Bretnor, Reginald, A KILLING IN SWORDS (Steve Lewis)	6:31
Brett, Simon, STAR TRAP (Steve Lewis)	5:27
Buchan, John, THE THIRTY-NINE STEPS (Martin Morse Wooster)	6:37
Bunn, Thomas, CLOSET BONES (Steve Lewis)	3:46
Burack, A.S., WRITING SUSPENSE AND MYSTERY FICTION (George Kelley)	2:39
Burke, J.F., THE KAMA SUTRA TANGO (Steve Lewis)	1:22
Butler, Ragan, CAPTAIN NASH AND THE WROTH INHERITANCE (Steve Lewis)	3:46
Butterworth, Michael, REMAINS TO BE SEEN (Steve Lewis)	4:35
Byfield, Barbara Ninde, FOREVER WILT THOU DIE (Steve Lewis)	5:32
Carr, John Dickson, THE SLEEPING SPHINX (Steve Lewis)	5:34
Chambers, Robert, THE NEON PREACHER (Steve Lewis)	3:45
Chase, James Hadley, CONSIDER YOURSELF DEAD (Theodore P. Dukeshire)	6:40
_____, MY LAUGH COMES LAST (Theodore P. Dukeshire)	3:51
Chastain, Thomas, VITAL STATISTICS (Steve Lewis)	3:44
Chesbro, George C., SHADOW OF A BROKEN MAN (George Kelley)	1:42
Cheyney, Peter, YOU CAN'T KEEP THE CHANGE (Stephen Mertz)	4:44
Clark, Gail, DULCIE BLIGH (Steve Lewis)	5:27

larke, Anna, THE LADY IN BLACK (Steve Lewis)	5:30
ollins, Max, THE SLASHER (George Kelley)	1:42
ollins, Michael, THE BLOOD-RED DREAMS (Steve Lewis)	1:27
_____, THE NIGHTRUNNERS (Steve Lewis)	6:33
opper, Basil, THE CURSE OF THE FLEERS (Amnon Kabatchnik)	1:35
_____, ditto (Steve Lewis)	3:46
_____, THE WEREWOLF (Amnon Kabatchnik)	4:46
ox, Richard, SAM 7 (Jeff Meyerson)	3:50
rispin, Edmund, THE MOVING TOYSHOP (Paul McCarthy)	1:43
ross, Amanda, THE QUESTION OF MAX (Myrtis Broset)	5:44
aly, Carroll John, MURDER FROM THE EAST (Theodore P. Dukeshire)	6:40
aniels, Les, THE BLACK CASTLE (Amnon Kabatchnik)	4:46
eighton, Len, THE BILLION DOLLAR BRAIN (Myrtis Broset)	1:38
_____, AN EXPENSIVE PLACE TO DIE (Myrtis Broset)	1:39
_____, HORSE UNDER WATER (Myrtis Broset)	5:44
elman, David, THE NICE MURDERERS (Steve Lewis)	1:22
elving, Michael, THE CHINA EXPERT (Steve Lewis)	1:24
errick, Lionel, DEVINE DEATH (Steve Lewis)	1:26
exter, Colin, THE SILENT WORLD OF NICHOLAS QUINN (Steve Lewis)	2:34
ickinson, Peter, WALKING DEAD (Steve Lewis)	5:27
onahue, Jack, THE LADY LOVED TOO WELL (Steve Lewis)	5:28
rummond, June, SLOWLY THE POISON (Steve Lewis)	1:29
llin, Stanley, THE LUXEMBOURG RUN (Steve Lewis)	3:44
_____, ditto (Francis M. Nevins, Jr.)	5:36
stes, Winston M., A SIMPLE ACT OF KINDNESS (Myrtis Broset)	3:56
errars, E.X., THE PRETTY PINK SHROUD (Myrtis Broset)	6:41
inney, Jack, THE NIGHT PEOPLE (Steve Lewis)	3:41
ish, Robert L., KEK HUUYGENS, SMUGGLER (Martin Morse Wooster)	5:41
leishman, A.S., SHANGHAI FLAME (Steve Lewis)	4:30
leming, Joan, EVERY INCH A LADY (Steve Lewis)	6:32
ollet., James, CROWN COURT (Steve Lewis)	6:32
oote-Smith, Elizabeth, NEVER SAY DIE (Steve Lewis)	1:24
oxx, Jack, DEAD RUN (Steve Lewis)	4:34
reeborn, Brian, TEN DAYS, MISTER CAIN? (Steve Lewis)	6:32
reemantle, Brian, CHARLIE M (Steve Lewis)	3:41
remlin, Celia, THE SPIDER-ORCHID (Steve Lewis)	6:30
ardner, John, TO RUN A LITTLE FASTER (Theodore P. Dukeshire)	6:41
arve, Andrew, THE LONG SHORT CUT (Jane S. Bakerman)	5:35
ash, Jonathan, THE JUDAS PAIR (Steve Lewis)	3:47
iles, Raymond, SHAMUS (Joe Lansdale)	3:53
ordon, Alex, THE CYPHER (Steve Lewis)	4:32
ores, Joe, GONE, NO FORWARDING (Francis M. Nevins, Jr.)	4:39
_____, ditto (Steve Lewis)	5:28
rant, C.L., THE HOUR OF THE OXRUN DEAD (Steve Lewis)	3:41
rant, Maxwell, FINGERS OF DEATH (Steve Lewis)	1:26
added, C.A., OPERATION APRICOT (Amnon Kabatchnik)	4:45
all, F.H., THE LAMB WHITE DAYS (Myrtis Broset)	1:36
alliday, Brett, MICHAEL SHAYNE'S LONG CHANCE (Steve Lewis)	4:32
arper, David, THE HANGED MEN (Myrtis Broset)	3:54
_____, THE PATCHWORK MAN (Myrtis Broset)	5:44
arris, Timothy, KYD FOR HIRE (Theodore P. Dukeshire)	3:52
arrison, William, HELL'S FULL (Myrtis Broset)	6:42
artshorne, THE MEXICAN ASSASSIN (Steve Lewis)	6:30
awkins, Willard E., THE COWLED MENACE (Steve Lewis)	4:35
ead, Lee, THE CRYSTAL CLEAR CASE (Steve Lewis)	3:43
enaghan, Jim, AZOR! (Steve Lewis)	3:45
ill, Headon, THE NARROWING CIRCLE (Charles Shibuk)	5:38
ill, Reginald, RULING PASSION (Steve Lewis)	3:42
ilton, John Buxton, DEAD-NETTLE (Steve Lewis)	5:26
immel, Richard, I HAVE GLORIA KIRBY (Steve Lewis)	5:34
_____, THE TWENTY-THIRD WEB (Amnon Kabatchnik)	4:45

Hinkle, Vernon, MUSIC TO MURDER BY (Myrtis Broset)	5:44
Hoch, Edward D., ed., BEST DETECTIVE STORIES OF THE YEAR--1977 (Steve Lewis)	1:21
_____, THE THEFTS OF NICK VELVET (Martin Morse Wooster)	6:39
Holton, Leonard, A CORNER OF PARADISE (Steve Lewis)	1:22
Homes, Geoffrey, THE MAN WHO MURDERED GOLIATH (Theodore P. Dukeshire)	5:43
_____, THE MAN WHO MURDERED HIMSELF (Theodore P. Dukeshire)	5:42
Household, Geoffrey, HOSTAGE: LONDON (Guy M. Townsend)	3:50
_____, RED ANGER (Guy M. Townsend)	2:40
_____, ROGUE MALE (Guy M. Townsend)	2:40
_____, WATCHER IN THE SHADOWS (Guy M. Townsend)	2:40
Hughes, Dorothy B., ERLE STANLEY GARDNER: THE CASE OF THE REAL PERRY MASON (Francis M. Nevins, Jr.)	4:37
Hull, Richard, A MATTER OF NERVES (Charles Shibuk)	4:42
Hutton, J(oy) P(erris), TOO GOOD TO BE TRUE (Charles Shibuk)	1:47
Innes, Michael, THE CASE OF SONIA WAYWARD (Steve Lewis)	6:35
_____, HONEYBATH'S HAVEN (Steve Lewis)	5:29
Jackson, Jon A., THE DIEHARD (Steve Lewis)	1:25
Jagoda, Robert, A FRIEND IN DEED (Steve Lewis)	4:33
James, P.D., DEATH OF AN EXPERT WITNESS (Jane S. Bakerman)	2:36
_____, ditto (Steve Lewis)	3:47
Jones, Elwyn, BARLOW EXPOSED (Steve Lewis)	3:42
Judson, William, KILMAN'S LANDING (Bill Crider)	5:40
Kaminsky, Stuart, BULLET FOR A STAR (Steve Lewis)	1:25
_____, ditto (James Jobst)	1:44
_____, MURDER ON THE YELLOW BRICK ROAD (Steve Lewis)	6:32
Keating, H.R.F., AGATHA CHRISTIE: FIRST LADY OF CRIME (Amnon Kabatchnik)	1:32
Kendrick, Tony, STEALING LILLIAN (James Jobst)	1:45
Lamb, Hugh, ed., THE TASTE OF FEAR (Steve Lewis)	1:28
Laumer, Keith, FAT CHANCE (Myrtis Broset)	3:55
Law, Janice, GEMINI TRIP (Steve Lewis)	1:26
Le Fanu, J.S., UNCLE SILAS: A TALE OF BARTRAM-HAUGH (Donna Balopole)	1:45
Lemarchand, Elizabeth, STEP IN THE DARK (Steve Lewis)	1:23
Leonard, Elmore, THE HUNTED (Myrtis Broset)	1:35
Lovesey, Peter, WAXWORK (Steve Lewis)	6:32
Lutz, John, BONEGRINDER (Steve Lewis)	4:36
McCloy, Helen, THE IMPOSTER (Steve Lewis)	1:24
MacDonald, John D., ONE FEARFUL YELLOW EYE (Amnon Kabatchnik)	4:47
Macdonald, Ross, LEW ARCHER, PRIVATE INVESTIGATOR (Amnon Kabatchnik)	4:47
McGerr, Pat, THE SEVEN DEADLY SISTERS (Charles Shibuk)	2:38
MacKenzie, Donald, RAVEN AND THE KAMIKAZE (Steve Lewis)	4:36
Maling, Arthur, ed., WHEN LAST SEEN (Steve Lewis)	2:33
Marric, J.J., GIDEON'S DRIVE (Steve Lewis)	1:28
Marsh, Ngaio, DEATH AT THE BAR (Myrtis Broset)	1:40
_____, DEATH IN ECSTASY (Myrtis Broset)	1:37
_____, ENTER A MURDERER (Myrtis Broset)	3:54
_____, SCALES OF JUSTICE (Myrtis Broset)	1:38
Masterman, J.C., AN OXFORD TRAGEDY (Jeff Meyerson)	2:38
Middlemiss, Robert, THE PARROT MAN (David H. Doerrer)	2:40
Mitchell, Gladys, DEATH AT THE OPERA (Mary Ann Grochowski)	5:42
Mitchell, James, SMEAR JOB (Steve Lewis)	3:44
Morice, Anne, SCARED TO DEATH (Steve Lewis)	4:32
Moyes, Patricia, BLACK WIDOWER (Steve Lewis)	4:35
Muller, Marcia, EDWIN OF THE IRON SHOES (Steve Lewis)	3:48
Neely, Richard, LIES (Steve Lewis)	5:29
_____, NO CERTAIN LIFE (Steve Lewis)	5:31
Newman, G.F., YOU NICE BASTARD (Bob Adey)	2:37
Odlum, Jerome, THE MIRABILIS DIAMOND (Theodore P. Dukeshire)	5:43
Oppenheim, E. Phillips, THE GREAT IMPERSONATION (Guy M. Townsend)	3:49
Parker, Robert B., MORTAL STAKES (Larry L. French)	1:32
Patrick, Andrew, BARETTA (Myrtis Broset)	1:40
Patrick, Q., MURDER AT CAMBRIDGE (Theodore P. Dukeshire)	5:43
Patterson, James, THE SEASON OF THE MACHETE (Steve Lewis)	4:31

Philips, Judson, FIVE ROADS TO DEATH (Steve Lewis)	5:31
Platt, Kin, THE SCREWBALL KING MURDER (Steve Lewis)	6:33
Ponder, Patricia, MURDER FOR CHARITY (Myrtis Broset)	3:55
_____, ditto (Steve Lewis)	4:31
Pollock, Robert, LOOPHOLE: OR HOW TO ROB A BANK (James Jobst)	1:44
Portway, Christopher, ALL EXITS BARRED (Theodore P. Dukeshire)	3:52
Post, Melville Davisson, THE COMPLETE UNCLE ABNER (Martin Morse Wooster)	5: 9
Prather, Richard, FIND THIS WOMAN (Stephen Mertz)	1:47
Pronzini, Bill and Collin Wilcox, TWOSPOT (Bill Crider)	6:36
Queen, Ellery, ed., MASTERPIECES OF MYSTERY (Paul McCarthy)	1:43
_____, THE TRAGEDY OF X (Martin Morse Wooster)	4:40
_____, A STUDY IN TERROR (Jeff Meyerson)	3:56
Racina, Thom, SWEET REVENGE (Steve Lewis)	4:30
Raymond, Clifford, THE MEN ON THE DEAD MAN'S CHEST (Steve Lewis)	5:32
Reade, Bill, THE IBIZA SYNDICATE (Steve Lewis)	1:29
Rice, Craig, THE LUCKY STIFF (Theodore P. Dukeshire)	5:43
_____, THE SUNDAY PIGEON MURDERS (Theodore P. Dukeshire)	5:43
Rogers, Joel Townsley, THE RED RIGHT HAND (Mary Ann Grochowski)	5:42
Ronns, Edward (Edward S. Aarons), STATE DEPARTMENT MURDERS (Stephen Mertz)	1:48
Ross, Angus, THE AMPURIAS EXCHANGE (Steve Lewis)	1:25
Roscoe, Mike, ONE TEAR FOR MY GRAVE (Steve Lewis)	5:33
Rostand, Robert, A KILLING IN ROME (Theodore P. Dukeshire)	3:51
Roueché, Berton, FAGO (Steve Lewis)	3:43
Roy, Archie, DEADLIGHT (Theodore P. Dukeshire)	5:42
Russell, Martin, THE MAN WITHOUT A NAME (Steve Lewis)	3:42
Saberhagen, Fred, THE HOLMES-DRACULA FILE (Joe Lansdale)	6:37
Sanders, Lawrence, THE TANGENT FACTOR (Steve Lewis)	5:30
Sapir, Richard and Warren Murphy, THE DESTROYER #31: THE HEAD MEN (Steve Lewis)	4:33
Scott, Jack S., SHALLOW GRAVE (Guy M. Townsend)	4:45
Seymour, Gerald, HARRY'S GAME (James Jobst)	1:44
Shah, Diana K., THE MACKIN COVER (Steve Lewis)	2:34
Silverman, Robert, THE CUMBERLAND DECISION (Steve Lewis)	3:47
Simenon, Georges, MAIGRET AND THE HOTEL MAJESTIC (Amnon Kabatchnik)	5:40
Smith, Charles Merrill, REVEREND RANDOLLPH AND THE AVENGING ANGEL (Steve Lewis)	6:30
Solomon, Brad, THE GONE MAN (Steve Lewis)	2:35
Spain, John, DEATH IS LIKE THAT (Stephen Mertz)	4:44
Stagge, Jonathan, DEATH, MY DARLING DAUGHTERS (Steve Lewis)	4:32
Stephan, Leslie, MURDER R.F.D. (Steve Lewis)	5:27
Symons, Julian, THE MAN WHO LOST HIS WIFE (Paul McCarthy)	1:43
Taschdigian, Claire, THE PEKING MAN IS MISSING (Steve Lewis)	2:33
Thomas, Jim, CROSS PURPOSES (Theodore P. Dukeshire)	6:41
Thompson, Estelle, FIND A CROOKED SIXPENCE (Steve Lewis)	5:26
Todd, Peter, THE ADVENTURES OF HERLOCK SHOLMES (Martin Morse Wooster)	5:41
Toepfer, Ray Grant, ENDPLAY (Steve Lewis)	1:29
Trevor, Elleston, THE THETA SYNDROME (Amnon Kabatchnik)	1:34
Tuska, Jon, THE DETECTIVE IN HOLLYWOOD (Francis M. Nevins, Jr.)	4:38
Uhnak, Dorothy, THE INVESTIGATION (Jane S. Bakerman)	1:41
van de Wetering, Janwillem, THE JAPANESE CORPSE (Steve Lewis)	5:28
_____, ditto (Myrtis Broset)	6:41
Wainright, John, POOL OF TEARS (Steve Lewis)	3:43
Watson, Colin, CHARITY ENDS AT HOME (Steve Lewis)	6:34
Way, Peter, DIRTY TRICKS (Steve Lewis)	4:31
West, Elliot, THE KILLING KIND (Steve Lewis)	4:33
Whitney, Phyllis A., MYSTERY OF THE ANGRY IDOL (Steve Lewis)	6:34
Wilcox, Colin, DOCTOR, LAWYER.... (Steve Lewis)	1:23
_____, THE WATCHER (Steve Lewis)	5:29
Wilden, Theodore, TO DIE ELSEWHERE (Steve Lewis)	1:29
Williams, David, TREASURE BY DEGREES (Steve Lewis)	5:26
_____, UNHOLY WRIT (Steve Lewis)	1:21

Williamson, Sherman, THE GLORY GAME (Steve Lewis) — 4:30
Wilmot, Robert Patrick, BLOOD IN YOUR EYE (Steve Lewis) — 1:30
Wilson, Jacqueline, MAKING HATE (Steve Lewis) — 6:33
Winslow, Pauline Glen, THE WITCH WILL MURDERS (Steve Lewis) — 1:22
Witting, Clifford, LET X BE THE MURDERER (Charles Shibuk) — 4:43
Wood, H.F., THE PASSENGER FROM SCOTLAND YARD (Steve Lewis) — 5:30
Wren, M.K., OH, BURY ME NOT (Steve Lewis) — 5:32

(*continued from page 45*) lating at an alarming rate, we feel quite content to sit back and allow Dame Agatha to have her way with us.

The cast is a good one--more stars than you can shake a live cobra at (yes, that, too)--and the only notable weakness is Lois Chiles as the new Mrs. Doyle. But she is soon excused from the proceedings--a bullet in the head--and thus justice is done in that respect, too.

This is a fine film for moviegoers seeking a few hours of diversion--designed by a very talented writer and acted out by very good players. So, if you can adjust to the slow, majestic pace of the great river itself, chances are that "Death on the Nile" will deliver you satisfied into port.

MYSTERY*FILE

SHORT REVIEWS BY STEVE LEWIS

Francis M. Nevins, Jr., *Corrupt and Ensnare* (Putnam's, 1978).
Deeply involved in lawyer-detective Loren Mensing's second mystery adventure are a contested will, a multi-million-dollar corporation with a history of working hand-in-glove with the CIA, and the not yet extinguished brand of ultra-liberalism left over from the 1960's. It begins with a shoebox full of money found in an old friend's study after his death, raising a pair of unanswered questions: Had the judge really once accepted a bribe influencing one of his court decisions, and if so, why?
If you like your detective puzzles rigorously tough, the tangled plot Nevins has in store for you is intended to challenge your little grey cells to the limit. Now and then there is a regrettable emphasis on the overdramatic and the bizarre, but there's a lot of punch packed into these pages, and it's a reading experience that shouldn't be missed. (B plus) * (Reviews so marked have appeared earlier in the Hartford *Courant*.)

Margaret Scherf, *The Beaded Banana* (Doubleday/Crime Club, 1978).
The title sounds like that of a second-rate rock group, but it's actually the prized possession of a member of the fly-by-night movie company that's shooting on location in Summerfield, Montana. An undesirable Las Vegas element is moving into town as well, and some unsavory political hijinx foreshadow some very strange things about to happen, including mur'er.
The detective is retired pathologist Dr. Grace Severance, and it's no reflection on her to say that what we have here is a mystery full of flutzy old ladies doing their thing. The humor is of the quiet zinger type, which does a lot to mitigate all the conclusions that are so ungracefully leapt to along the way. (B minus)*

Dan Greenburg, *Love Kills* (Harcourt Brace Jovanovich, 1978).
Except for the unmistakable Greenburg touch, this is a perfectly ordinary mystery novel. What he has accomplished, however, is the transformation of the dull clay of genre fiction into a brilliantly sparkling mosaic of life and death in the modern world, revealing as he does so the innermost secrets of the urban jungles that all too many of today's cities cannot begin to cover over with tacky glitter or a barrage of glowing press releases.
It begins with the first of a series of murdered young women, living alone in Manhattan with no real attachments, then a young Jewish cop's first tour of the city morgue since joining Homicide, followed by an equally young Catholic girl's psychic vision of the next of the killings yet to come. The killer is motivated by love, not hatred, not that it makes any difference in the end. Finding it difficult to initiate any kind of relationship with females on a normal basis, he instead watches them from his apartment windows through theirs, follows them to the drugstore and the supermarket, rummages through their garbage on the street, in short does a job getting to know them without ever meeting them that the FBI would be justifiably proud of, before turning up on their doorstep for an unannounced first date.

In the meantime, the cop, named Max Seegal, has met Babette, the girl with the dreams, and of his dreams, and whether he believes in her talent at first or not, their romance, filled with dialogue that would charm all but the most confirmed misanthrope, blossoms and blooms in the midst of a constant flurry of hyperactive policework. When Babette's stepfather makes improper advances toward her one evening while her mother is absent, she moves out and in with Max, most refreshingly innocent of ulterior intentions, most surprising in these days of X-rated movies and liberated heroines of easy virtue, and in vivid contrast to the detailed sex kinks exhibited by the killer in the final moments in the lives of those he loves.

His identity remains unknown until the final chapters, by the way, so while his final attempt to add yet another victim to his growing list can be seen coming from mid-book on, this is a book that can be read solely as a who-done-it kind of detective story.

But not by anyone with the least bid of empathy for his or her fellow beings. Seldom can a book have you laughing, crying, shivering in suspense and cringing in fear--all at the same time. Greenburg, the author of such previous books as *How to Be a Jewish Mother* and *Scoring: A Sexual Memoir*, delineates all levels of urban society with a touch that's utterly delightful, from the M.E. who lords it over his dismal domain on the basement floor of the city morgue, the boogie-hating doorman of the first victim's apartment building, Seegal's crudely bigoted partner in Homicide, the fading beauty of the killer's Arthur Murray dancing instructor, to all of the defenseless young single women who prided themselves on being so able to take care of themselves in an uncaring city filled with terror.

This is nearly as perfect as a thrilling and gripping work of fiction can be. There'll be no valid excuse for missing this one! (A plus)*

Bartholomew Gill, *McGarr and the Sienese Conspiracy* (Scribner's, 1977; 186 pp.).
What's an Irish police inspector doing in Italy guarding the head of British Intelligence? The explanation is not very satisfying, nor is much of this tale, overly cluttered with historic background and gourmet meals. It's the kind of book more in favor with critics than with readers, imbued with the merest breath of life. (F)

Hugh Pentecost, *The Steel Palace* (Dodd Mead, 1977; 188 pp.).
If the stories about the last days of Howard Hughes weren't (apparently) true, no one could possibly believe this as fiction. When public relations expert Julian Quist takes a million dollar job for an enormously wealthy recluse about to open a mammoth hotel-casino in Atlantic City, his nose for trouble smells something crooked cooking, and suddenly Quist and his lovely lady friend Lydia find themselves prisoners in the near-empty complex. The only other guest is the jovial dictator of a newly emerged African state, but at this point survival is more important than diplomatic niceties. Pentecost's writing style is awfully pulpy, but the pages that flashed by had me climbing the walls in exuberant suspense. (A plus)

Geroge Hardinge, ed., *Winter's Crimes 9* (St. Martins, 1978).

The contents page, and for that maeter, the front cover, is a veritable who's who of contemporary British mystery writers. Not all of these authors are well known in this country, yet, but in along with the less familiar names are ones like Geoffrey Household, Patricia Highsmith, and Ruth Rendell that are known to mystery readers everywhere. The twelve stories here are originals, written especially for this collection, but even if they had been scoured up as the best of the year from everywhere else, they could hardly be of any greater quality. What we're given is in fact a cross-section of current crime fiction, with tales ranging from the pure detective puzzle proposed by Colin Dexter to the subtle domestic affair tinged with bitter irony that James McClure writes about, in which crime has only the most tenuous connection. A definite must for fans of the short story. (B plus)*
NOTE: For the record, the other authors are: Celia Dale, Elizabeth Ferrars, Derek Robinson, John Wainwright, Martin Woodhouse, Margaret Yorke, and P.B. Yuill.

Michael T. Hinkemeyer, *The Fields of Eden* (Putnam's, 1977).
Tragedy hits a small Minnesota town as the wife and children of a young minister are found brutally murdered. The key to the crime is sex, in conflict with religion, coarsely stated, and a theme built in stark contrast to the antics of the squabbling sheriff's department and the unheard of courtroom procedures used to break the case. While it's hard to believe that St. Cloud is so little removed from the days of the frontier, there is still no doubt that Hinkemeyer tells a compelling story. Most of the story potential produced by the pressures and inner torments facing Sheriff Whippletree seems to have been exhausted, but one is left with the strong desire to meet him again soon. (B plus)

Linda J. LaRosa & Barry Tanenbaum, *The Random Factor* (Doubleday, 1978; 273 pp.).
Four men, bored with backgammon and simple puzzles in logic, turn to a game of random killings played with the entire population of New York City as pawns. Their main adversary, after the manpower and crime-solving expertise of the NYPD fails, is famed criminologist Noah Aikman, whose specialty is in making connections between apparently unconnected scraps of information.
Behind the madness of random murders is indeed a pattern, one presented as a blood-splattered challenge to the reader as well. One only wonders how close to the edge of this kind of craziness a city can really be, and what kind of human race it is that makes this sort of story possible, but considering recent headlines it's easy for the authors to be chillingly convincing. Another jarring note comes as the pursuer makes an important move as ruthlessly as his quarry--aren't good guys always supposed to wear white hats? (A minus)*

George C. Chesbro, *City of Whispering Stone* (Simon & Schuster, 1978; 236 pp.).
Ladies and gentlemen, presenting Bob Frederickson, alias Mongo the Magnificent, former circus dwarf with a Ph.D. in criminology, now moonlighting as the world's shortest private detective!
This case of the missing Iranian weight-lifter is actually Mongo's second, and it takes him deep into the web of revolution threatening that ancient oil-rich kingdom as it struggles

to make its way into this century. Plenty of bodies pile up, and lots of double (and redoubled) agents, but as in cheap carnival sideshows, the emphasis seems to be more on flash than substance. Cotton candy also comes to mind. (C)*

Jack S. Scott, *The Shallow Grave* (Harper & Row, 1977; 188 pp.).
As a writer, Scott nicely captures the rich, earthy flavor and beauty of the English countryside--if only, as someone's sure to have said in such instances, the characters didn't insist on getting in the way!
Inspector Rosher is a coarse bloke, through and through, and the personality conflict between him and his flu-ridden chief superintendent puts them both through never-ceasing torment. Working together on this case of the murdered young school teacher, they do quite a wretched job of investigation. Justice does prevail, but only of its own accord. Scott himself seems to look on with disgust, then with pity, but then also with sad insight, which surprises as well as pleases. (B)*

John Buxton Hilton, *Some Run Crooked* (St. Martin's, 1978).
Hilton is making a fine career of telling tales of murder taking place through the ages in the English hill country of Derbyshire. Here's another. As it happens, this one's from but twenty years ago, and yet the death of the young girl who comes to Peak Low to be married is a fate soon seen to be more than coincidentally connected to the two identical murders from the past that the area is famous for.
More than usual, the investigation that follows is a struggle with lies, both innocent and deliberate, complicated by failing memories and a town's unswerving loyalty to its own. A certain amount of contrivance has to be granted this time, keeping the effort from the level established by some of Hilton's previous excursions into history, but it's still unquestionably a compelling story of down-to-earth detection. (B)*

Rex Burns, *Speak for the Dead* (Harper & Row, 1978; 249 pp.).
After appearing in two books as a valuable member of Denver's narcotics squad, detective Gabe Wager has been switched to homicide detail. This is hardly surprising, for if the series is to continue, how many interesting stories of the dope rackets are there to tell? What's not expected is the lone-wolfe approach Wager is allowed to employ on this, his first murder case, and a bizarre on at that, involving the head of a beautiful model found picturesquely abandoned in the city's botanical gardens. In all other details the life of a dedicated cop rings true, in stark contrast to what's seen every evening on every TV screen in the country, but it should also be noted that a large part of a policeman's daily activity is strictly wearisome routine. (C plus)*

Jane Langton, *The Memorial Hall Murder* (Harper & Row, 1978).
All mystery readers who are fond of New England backgrounds surely have met Homer Kelly by now, that ex-assistant DA now retired to a life in Concord meant to be sedentary, except that this now makes three cases of murder that have arisen to challenge his infallible (though sometimes fumbling) investigative finger.
Harvard's famed Memorial Hall is the scene of a bombing in this one, and in the blast the conductor of the school's Collegium Musicum abruptly loses his head. Langton knows her way around Harvard Square, and during the following semester we're

led on a merry tour from the highest steepletop down to the depths of the bedrock far below. Her version of internal university politics is less sure, but it's a handy target and it stays a constant source of lively amusement. In fact, the whole charade, climaxing with a rousing rendition of Handel's *Messiah*, is really quite mad and utterly unbelievable, and paradoxically is all the more charming for it! (B)*

Al Bird, *Murder So Real* (Coward, McCann & Geoghegan, 1978).

Sinclair Lewis Maxwell starts out as a fairly likable new character, a reporter with a suitably sour-tough view of the world, content in finding a refuge from it by hanging out on the pages of the sports section. Until, that is, his girl friend, who'd been working on an exclusive exposé of some mobile home cathouses rolling up and down the Calfornia freeway system, is shot to death in her bedroom.

Finding the man responsible is easy enough, but when he decides that it's up to him to mete out a revenge that the law cannot, the story backs up into a series of shady financial manipulations that Maxwell hopes will bring the man's shaky financial empire to its knees. What's surprising is that in spite of all Maxwell's efforts, he's just not very good at it. When the characters are so inadequately prepared for the parts they're asked to play, it's awfully hard as well to fight trends in detective fiction over a century old. (C plus)*

Michael Butterworth, *X Marks the Spot* (Doubleday/Crime Club, 1978; 183 pp.).

A brilliantly outrageous scheme to kidnap the final remains of Karl Marx, left unguarded all these years in a London tomb, succeeds, and with a surprising amount of ease. The bodysnatchers hope to auction the bones off as relics to the Communist faithful around the world, but alas, the likable group of thieves who pull off the first part of the job are all too obviously in over their heads. Too late they learn that far more dangerous predators lie in wait for just such amateurs as themselves to come along.

Here's a book as much pleasant fun to read as anything's been in recent months, yet there's still an uneasy feeling afterwards that a more satisfying conclusion should have been arranged. (B plus)*

Tony Scaduto, *A Terrible Time to Die* (Putnam's, 1978; 204 pp.).

When a reporter goes after a story he's ninety percent sure will never see print, he's nothing more than our old friend, the self-employed private eye driven solely by an overdeveloped sense of moral outrage. Dead is the mayor's brother-in-law, shot to death in his library, and at one time a friend.

The evidence points to suicide, but some Mafia connections and other unsavory matters are involved, and the not-so-grieving widow does not believe it. Deceptively non-gripping throughout, but the story nevertheless does find a unique way of prevailing. (B plus)*

Gladys S. Gallant, *Living Image* (Doubleday, 1978; 185 pp.).

With a storm of unanswered questions ringing through her brain, Edity Weston returns to New York from Paris to try to discover why her sister had apparently committed suicide just after writing her for the first time in ten years. Almost at once her search leads her into close contact with several of the many men in Karen's life, and her story quickly becomes a fashionably complicated novel of romance straight from the ladies' magazines.

For mystery lovers, however, plenty of sinister menace does develope when she's persuaded to impersonate her dead sister in a foolhardy attempt to learn the truth. Detective fans are challenged to solve the puzzle as well, but some of the more difficult pieces probably will have to be held until the final chapter before they can finally be put into place. (B plus)*

Edwin Gage, *Phoenix No More* (Harper & Row, 1978; 200 pp.).
Arizona is being rapidly Californicated, and a building contractor rebelling against the system disappears, even though former D.A.'s investigator Daniel Falconer has been hired as his bodyguard. Bribes, kickbacks, and "short work" on the part of engineers and the construction industry mean millions of dollars of untaxed profits, even when it comes to building a new nuclear facility in the state.

In terms of the enormous problem of disposing of nuclear waste, Gage paints a damningly bleak picture that leaves no room for compromise. This is a tough detective story as well, told with unusual intensity; the strong implication is that we're nothing but wisps of straw being blown hither and yon by the wind. A fine job. (A)*

Michael Barak, *The Enigma* (Morrow, 1978; 240 pp.).
From the title you might be thinking that this book is just another of the many others in the recent deluge of occult fiction that publishers seem to be pushing off onto us mystery readers. Ah, but no, it's not that sort of thing at all. What it is instead is yet another espionage thriller taking place during World War II, the heyday of English spydom, when the tides of history could still be turned by the fforts of single men. And the Enigma? The German enciphering and deciphering system, a bit of electronic wizardry that may very well have been Hitler's most jealously guarded secret.

Nor is it entirely fictitious, either. Maybe you've already read Winterbotham's book on the activities of British Intelligence during the war. Barak goes on from there and supposes the availability of a supreme international adventurer, the self-styled Baron de Belvoir. Under extreme duress he's sent into occupied Paris; his assignment, to obtain an Enigma machine under non-suspicious circumstances and facilitate the Allies' landing in Normandy.

To the Baron, here's a challenge for the thrill of it. To the reader, here's real-for-goodness pulp writing, with the same driving readability. Include the obligatory torture scene, an internal anti-Nazi conspiracy, plus a beautiful Jewish girl and a twist of *Carmen*, and even though you may care for -ar stories only about as much as I do, you might go for this one. (B)
NOTE TO HOLMESIANS: Since British Intelligence works here out of a commandeered department store on Baker Street, there is a hint of Irregularity, almost enough to be worth a mention, don't you think?

Bill Pronzini & Collin Wilcox, *Twospot* (Putnam's, 1978).
Collaborations between mystery story writers involving each of their separate detective character creations are surprisingly uncommon, but working together on this case that be-

gins with the son of a California winemaking family who's worried about the romantic entanglements of his widowed mother are both Pronzini's famous no-name private detective and Wilcox's Lt. Hastings, of San Francisco Homicide.

Both normally tell their own story in first person, and that's how the book is split up, giving us a brief but welcome glimpse of each as seen through the eyes of the other. They're remarkably alike, each with personal problems now relegated to the past, both with inner commitments requiring right to prevail over wrong. The collaboration also produces a splendid combination of detective puzzle and suspense thriller, one that races to a room-shattering climax, particularly so for readers slow in putting together all the pieces.

Incidentally, the nameless private eye now has a first name. It's Bill, of course. (A minus)*

V. C. Clinton-Baddeley, *My Foe Outstretch'd Beneath the Tree* (Arrow, 1968; Arrow paperback edition, 1974; 192 pp.).

Once in a while I slip up and don't get around to writing one of these reviews right after finishing a book, as I should. This I read a couple of weeks ago, and I'm afraid I don't remember all that I should about it, other than I definitely meant to recommend it, highly and enthusiastically.

Some non-fading impressions remain. The detective is semi-retired academician R. V. Davie, now in his 70s, but he's assuredly still of keen and clever wit, with the pleasantly sardonic view of the world that the elderly are most entitled to. The mystery has something to do with a murdered fellow club member, a jealous husband, the opera, and some tapes produced by the English Department of a small college. A good deal of time-tabling goes on--and aren't you also always glad when a detective takes the trouble to make lists in order to sort out and arrange his thoughts?

At one time, quite early, I remember finding a clue that convinced me I knew who did it. When you come to it, just remember that it's probably not that easy. You may have a few dozen people you're sure who did it before you're done. As a detective, Davie is dapper and delightful, and the mystery's both delicious and destrously deceitful. What more can you ask? (A)

June Thompson, *Death Cap* (Doubleday/Crime Club, 1973; first U.S. edition 1977; 187 pp.).

When the police receive an annonymous letter suggesting that a case of mushroom poisoning might be something other than a simple accident, the problem, as always, is twofold: Who is the killer, and who wrote the note? Residents of small English villages seem to possess more than their share of human frailties for criminal investigations to uncover, as Detective Inspector Rudd knows full well. There are undercurrents and roots to the past that only local townsfolk know and understand, and it takes a great deal of painstaking work before the question of guilt can begin to be properly resolved.

Thompson does not write with the determined forcefullness of a P.D. James, nor does she exhibit the strong sense of irony of a Ruth Rendell, but she does possess a hint of pathos all her own--and how surprising it is that it occurs so seldom in mystery novels, considering the true nature of the crime of murder. It makes this particular story, at least, all the more likable for it, and it makes us quite content as well when justice wins out once again in the end. (B plus)

VERDICTS

(MORE REVIEWS)

Mickey Spillane, *The Twisted Thing* (E.P. Dutton, 1966).
   There's an interesting history behind this book. According to the library reference work *Contemporary Authors*, which is based on questionnaires filled out by the authors themselves, Spillane originally write this (his working title was *For Whom the Gods Would Destroy*) "about 1947", although it was not published until 1966. It's easy to see why. This is very weak Spillane and third-rate Mike Hammer.
   In the beginning, Spillane had a narrative power which was all his own. But he was a very derivative plotter and stylist whose main inspiration was the popular Race Williams private eye series by Carroll John Daly which appeared in books and pulp magazines throughout the '20s, '30s and '40s. In his first published novel, *I, the Jury* (1947), Spillane renamed Williams, Hammer, adapted Daly's style of characterization and general feel, and simply added a strong vengeance motif, which Daly usually shied away from, and graphic (for the time) sex, which had always been *verbotten* in the pulps. *I, the Jury* went on to become a best seller while Daly's career declined with the folding of the pulps in the early '50s. Although Spillane openly acknowledged his debt to Daly, there was some justification to Daly's bitterness and feeling that he had been ripped off. By the early '50s, with his best work such as *The Big Kill*, Spillane had matured into a strongly individualized talent in his own right, realizing the full potential of both the Hammer character and the vengeance storyline. But all of the negative criticisms which apply to *Jury* are also applicable to *The Twisted Thing*: it's a crude, overly imitative work by a beginning writer still feeling his way, and it's amazing that more critics haven't remarked on the wide gap in quality between it and Spillane's more mature work of the sixties, such as the Tiger Mann novels.
   In addition to its organic weakness, all kinds of things keep this from being a very good Mike Hammer story. Most of the book takes place outside of Ner York City. Spillane is to New York what Chandler is to L.A. or Hammer to Hollywood. His books are as much about the city itself as the people in it and what they're doing to each other. Then, this is one of the few books wherein Hammer is actually working on a case for a client. As a bloodthirsty, vengeance-mad modern day Conan, Mike Hammer is one of the most powerful, effectively drawn characters in the private eye genre. As a private *detective* he ranks only slightly above Al Capp's Fearless Fosdick when it comes to picking up clues and putting solutions together, and that's what he's supposed to be doing here. Spillane just can't write that way and Hammer "solves" this case by some of the wildest guesses and most glaring coincidences in crime fiction.
   Actually, the plot's basic premise is a good one. A scientist, as part of a long range experiment, is raising his otherwise normal fourteen year old son to be a genius. Suddenly the boy is kidnapped. Hammer rescues the boy early in the book without nabbing the kidnappers. Then the scientist is murdered and things are quickly complicated by a house full of greedy, plotting heirs and a sadistic cop who runs the small town and hates Hammer's guts. The story has more twists

than a Raymond Chandler novel but unfortunately the plot's considerable potential is effectively sabotaged by a "solution" that makes barely an iota of sense, lame dialogue, sleazy, gratuitous sex and all of the other offenses already itemized.

The Twisted Thing is an interesting bibliographic oddity, but with ten other Hammer novels to choose from--most of them displaying Spillane at the top of his form--I'd definitely recommend saving this one for last. (Stephen Mertz)

James Atlee Phillips, *Pagoda* (Macmillan, 1951; Bantam, 1952).
When I read Philip Atlee's *The Green Wound* (GM, 1963), I thought I'd discovered a new series hero. I was wrong. The first-person narrator of *The Green Wound*, Joe Gall, had already been around for more than ten years. He is also the protagonist of *Pagota*. Though this latter book is written in the third person, Gall is still recognizably Gall, and the style is just as cryptic as in the first-person stories that came along later, under a slightly different name.

The story is a cynical one. Gall goes to Burma to run an airline flying goods for both sides in a civil war. He's paid a huge sum of money, but it doesn't appear that he'll ever live to spend it. People start dying all around him, and the conspiracy begins to unravel. But as anyone who's read the Gall books knows, Joe is a survivor. His loyalty, in the final analysis, is to himself. As he tells another character in *Pagoda*. "The trouble with us is that we're a couple of businessmen completely surrounded by patriots." This is the attitude that seems to sustain Gall in all his adventures.

This book is very short (120 pages in the Bantam edition); the writing is terse. If you've followed Gall's career lately but wondered what he was doing in the old days, you owe it to yourself to look this one up. (Bill Crider)

Charlotte Armstrong, *Seven Seats to the Moon* (Coward-McCann, 1969).
Charlotte Armstrong has acquired a sizeable following of readers who, over the past twenty years or so, have come to admire her special type of suspense novel. Unfortunately, I haven't been able to include myself in this group. Her early and much-praised *A Dram of Poison* I thought was not very well written and as such lacked the charm to overcome its general air of improbability. Now I've tried a 1969 Charlotte Armstrong and--alas!--find disappointment again.

A chap named J (no period) Middleton Little, from Burbank, California, finds himself in a Chicago hospital following a minor traffic mishap. He shares his room with a fellow named Barkis (a celebrated scientist incognito) who confides to him that the apocalypse is at hand and, since there will be a need for an "average family" among the proposed survivors who will escape anihilation on a new type of Ark, he is prepared to offer him "seven tickets to the moon". Our J Middle-(get it?)-ton Little would thus survive with six of his clan. Barkis later is removed from the picture when he commits suicide and now Mr. Goodrich begins dogging J (as Miss Armstrong calls him), trying to determine precisely what Barkis had let J in on.

J leaves the hospital and goes home, trailed by Goodrich. things are fairly slow-moving up to this point. Now they become diffuse and choppy. J's domestic situation is explored, his family members (numerous) brought into the picture, and their tensions and problems are now blended in with those related to J and Goodrich and another group that is busy counterspying Goodrich. These undercover folk insinuate themselves into J's family circle, the narrative focus begins shifting about wildly and quite arbitrarily away from J to various of these others and, well . . . . The one thing that could save all this mish-mash (in the absence of dead-seriousness, which Miss Armstrong isn't trying for) is a graceful light touch in the writing. Sorry, I didn't find it there. (Donald A. Yates)

Edward Boyd and Bill Knox, *The View from Daniel Pike* (Arrow, 1974).

Bill Knox is a writer who attracted my attention when he was first being published in the United States. Even though his mysteries were not intricate, they were bolstered by vivid descriptions of Scottish city and sea life. Recently I tried a retrospective look and tried to recapture the former enthusiasm, reading all the books under the name Knox as well as a few under the names of Macleod and Webster. Either I've grown more critical or the later Knoxes succumbed to malnourishment of the formula. In the earlier titles Webb Carrick (Chief Officer of a Fisheries cutter in the Hebrides) and Thane and Moss (a matched pair of 'tecs in Glasgow) maintain the interest and action comes quickly enough; latterly not enough has changed to make it worthwhile finishing. However, in the attempt to go through Knox's production, I did come up with a blessing and that's what this review is about.

In the midst of everything I found a paperback entitled *The View from Daniel Pike*, by Edward Boyd and Bill Knox. The title page reads, "Bill Knox, *The View from Daniel Pike*. From scripts by Edward Boyd, deviser of the BBC television series." Well, whoever wrote this book, it's a different cup of tea.... Here are five novellas (30 to 40 pages each) about Daniel Pike, who is much more like the West Coast (USA) tattered and torn worldly-wise private eye than he s like the basically proper and stiff upper lip Knox family of detectives.

When I read the opening sentences of "Good Morning, Yesterday", the first story in the book, I knew I had something good: "It wasn't the bailiffs who broke the lock on my office door. Old age did that and there's never seemed much sense in having it repaired. Locks mean you've something worth stealing . . . ." And thus we are introduced to Daniel Pike, Investigations and Debt Collections, who has a soft spot (the ONLY one) for a beautiful blind night club performer.

Pike talks in the clipped prose that lovers of the tough guy genre dote upon, directly out of Sam Spade and should have been played by Bogey, if the times had been right.

The five titles in this group are: "Good Morning, Yesterday"; "Four Walls"; "Philomena and the Tattie-Howkers"; "A Tale of Two Cities"; "A Slight Case of Absalom". Clearly the collaboration was a blessed one for these are the kind of stories that bring you in and carry you along. If you know of more let me know. (Howard Waterhouse)

Lou Cameron, *File on a Missing Redhead* (Gold Medal, 1968).

The paperback original can often offer many pleasant surprises to the seeker after merit.

The best of these works contain taut, well-constructed, and involving narratives that feature reasonably well-rounded characters. *File on a Missing Redhead* is a case in point.

Its opening is somewhat reminiscent of the police procedural form as Lieutenant Frank Talbot of the Las Vegas Police Department, who is also first person narrator, is summoned to an automobile wrecking yard to investigate the unidentified body of a red-haired woman found in the trunk compartment of a car slated for the hydraulic press.

Talbot seeks to identify the girl, but the author complicates his job by injecting such elements as a skip-tracing agency with a missing (and ingenuous) redhead, an old flame of Talbot's whose current and jealous *inamorato* is enjoying a long vacation at the state's expense, an almost professional credit-jumper whose other flaws include excessive gambling, satyriasis, and homicidal mania, and the brutal dynamite-murder of Talbot's driver into the narrative.

There are also a few gangsters--several of the professional assassin variety, and many law enforcement officers to add spice to an already fast-paced story.

Talbot's quest turns into a long chase--with many detours-- for the above mentioned credit jumper who is menacing his ingenuous redheaded companion, and ends violently in a shootout at the face of an abandoned mine.

The author then proceeds to invoke the spirit of detection to show us that all was not as simple as it seemed to be, and then ends his narrative with a rather cruel and hard-boiled flourish that is completely unexpected. (Charles Shibuk)

Larry D. Names, *Twice Dead* (Leisure Books, 1978; $1.75).

The mystery of Lee Harvey Oswald has remained with us for over 15 years. Was Oswald the lone assassin of John F. Kennedy; did he have assistance in committing the crime; or was he merely a "patsy" set up to take the blame for the killing as Oswald himself insisted? Jack Ruby forever shrouded the whole affair in mystery when he shot and killed Oswald in the basement of the Dallas jail two days after JFK's murder.

After Oswald's murder, curious rumors began to circulate concerning Oswald's past. Several witnesses came forward to testify that Oswald had apparently appeared in public showing a belligerent and hostile attitude along with excellent rifle marksmanship, while records prove he was either with his family or at work. This seemed to indicate that there was more than one person claiming to be Lee Harvey Oswald in the Dallas area, maybe setting up the real Oswald to be a "patsy" in the assassination. Thus was born the Second Oswald Theory of JFK's assassination.

Twice Dead is a novel which concerns itself with the Second Oswald Theory. Tom Regan, an investigative reporter, is given puzzling information by his sister and her husband, an ex-marine who served with Lee Oswald in the Philippines in the late 1950's. This information seems to indicate that Oswald had a double in the Marines and that Oswald may have taken over the double's identity or vice versa after an assault incident in the Philippines. Regan is plunged into a maze of hidden identities and murders, all designed to cover up the infamous deed commited in Dallas' Dealey Plaza in 1963. The resulting adventure is a highly entertaining tale although some of the plot twists can be anticipated too easily. The book is well worth its purchase price and makes one ponder as to what really happened in Dallas on November 22, 1963, and who really was Lee Harvey Oswald--assassin or patsy or . . . ? (Thomas L. Motsinger)

Steven Whitney, *Singled Out* (Morrow; 261 pp.; $8.95); Dan Greenburg, *Love Kills* (Harcourt-Brace-Jovanovich; 277 pp.; $7.95).

Psychopathic killers, stalking their prey in the singles bars of Manhattan's upper east side, are the hero-villains of two new, chilling tales of unrelenting terror.

In *Singled Out*, David Cooper is your mother's dream. Handsome. Witty. Considerate. Affluent. He enjoys meeting attractive young women over drinks. Sometimes he takes them home and makes love to them, with passion and tenderness. Then he systematically mutilates their bodies with his collection of ice picks.

It isn't very long before police investigators link the grisly murders. They devise an unorthodox stakeout that relies on ten of New York's most courageous female cops, who frequent the bars, waiting to be picked up by men who fit the killer's description. Each woman must then be charmed into the man's bedroom, while outside the apartment her partner, a male detective, stands ready in case of trouble.

Side-tracked by the love affair that develops between two of the police hunters, the proceedings still manage to build relentlessly into a nerve-wracking climax.

Love Kills by Dan Greenburg features the "hyena" who researches, follows, and, in frenzied succession, brutally murders a series of single women.

Rationalizing his diabolical crimes with the misguided conviction that he kills for love, the Hyena sets the city on edge. Numerous police precincts tirelessly chase wide-ranging, doubtful leads.

In the midst of the turmoil, Max Segal, a newcomer to the Homicide Division, is saddled with this toughest of cases. A bizarre turn of events finds him the confidante of a young woman whose psychic visions have convinced her that she is "tuned in" to the case. What follows is their round-the-clock search for the killer--a search which ultimately threatens their lives.

The grim events are lightened by humorous vignettes of ridiculous situations befalling police investigators on the wrong track.

Following in the footsteps of *Looking for Mr. Goodbar* by Judith Rossner and Faye Dunaway's movie *Eyes of Laura Mars*, both *Singled Out* and *Love Kills* are overlong and suffer from excess, unconvincing psychological manifestations. Nevertheless, the two works are spellbinding in their haunting intensity and manage to capture convincingly the dilemma of the lonely young women of today against the realistic backgrounds of a metropolitan city. (Amnon Kabatchnik)

Robert Ludlum, *The Gemini Contenders* (The Dial Press, 1976).

It is 1939. Hitler's war is spreading rapidly, uncontrollably through Europe. A mysterious chest is loaded onto a train in the dead of night somewhere in Greece to be spirited away into Mussolini's Italy. The chest has been buried for nearly 1500 years, the charge of a monastic order of militant monks who now fear that its incredible contents, documents dating back to the time of Christ, may fall into irresponsible hands. The documents question, and possibly disprove, the very theological foundations of the Catholic Church in particular and all Christian religions in general. The impact of the chest's contents could dwarf even the coming war, bringing such confusion to the world that, it is feared by the monks,

Hitler would have little trouble in exploiting the resulting chaos, ending the war victoriously practically before it has begun. And so the chest is buried; hidden somewhere in the vast reaches of the Italian Alps. But within days all who know of its new location are dead. . . .

That is the opening and premise of Robert Ludlum's long, very effective novel of suspense, which follows the attempts of the Nazis, the Vatican, the monks and many others to locate the chest over the next thirty-four years, killing and double- and triple-corssing each other endlessly in the process. (Yes, there are even some homicidal priests and cardinals running about.)

This was the first bona fide "Bestseller" (16 weeks on the NY *Times* listing) that I've read in some time. It's easy to see how Ludlum, a former actor, has attained such status. The book is a good one.

It has been said that most writers are either good stylists or good plotters; rarely both. This is certainly true in Ludlum's case. The book is flawed by a flat, oddly cliched pulp writing style ("With the speed born of a hundred fire fights, Fontine was on his haunches, the Berretta leveled, spitting bullets . . . "), and a complete absence of "feel" for any of the exotic locales portrayed. But boy! do things happen. Keep Things Moving is the name of Ludlum's game and he excells at piling plot twists and complications atop each other at a breathtaking rate, page after page, chapter after chapter. It's really quite impressive. He also has a fine knack for characterization, although the Gemini contenders of the title are, strangely, the weakest characters in the book. The plot does have some rough edges and the cilmax is telegraphed a good seventy pages in advance--the last third of the book is quite a bit weaker than the first two--but pace is everything here and all these flaws seem to whiz right by unnoticed at first as the pages keep turning.

Ludlum obviously set out to write a nonstop thriller, and succeeded admirably. (Stephen Mertz)

Michael Avallone, *The Doctor's Wife* (Beacon Signal pb #B626F, 1963).

Michael Avallone is best known for his 32 Ed Noon private eye books, yet his total output to date has been a whopping 133 titles, the majority of them paperback originals. These include gothics and potboiler novelizations of TV and movie scripts, but also include a number of non-series suspense novels. *The Doctor's Wife*, a hard to find item if there ever was one, is from this last group and is one of Avallone's best.

This one has all the spirit of a Noon novel and, in fact, hero Vince Allen is a dead ringer for the Manhattan Eye. Like Noon, he narrates his own story.

Vince, an out of work actor, is in Central Park one morning when he meets the meautiful, mysterious Erika. An innocent encounter. But they meet again the next morning. And the next. And soon Allen finds himself being drawn inexorably into the web of Erika's private life, her sinister European husband and their marital problems--problems which culminate in bloody murder.

Granted, the pivitol plot element is a wild coincidence. But the well-maintained pace, the fully dimensioned characters, the intriguing storyline and the supremely skillful, authoritative depiction of New York theater- and nightlife all add up to make this an A-1 effort.

Favorite line: "I was as mixed up as a tossed salad." (SM)

Edgar Box, *Three by Box* (Random House, $1295).

In the early 1950s, at the end of his first period as a novelist and the beginning of his career as a writer of live television drama, Gore Vidal turned briefly to the detective story. Under the pseudonym of Edgar Box he published a trilogy of mystery novels narrated by and starring Peter Cutler Sargeant II, young public relations expert, sexual gymnast (exclusively hetero), and amateur sleuth.

The books have been reprinted regularly in paperback over the past quarter century, often with a glowing encomium from Vidal himself emblazoned on their covers, and have now been reissued in a hardcover omnibus. Judged as formal detective novels all three are mediocre, but Vidal's guided tour through the worlds of art, politics and high society entertains us royally with countless gleefully sardonic jabs at every target in sight.

In *Death in the Fifth Position* (1952) Peter is hired to procure favorable media coverage for a ballet company which is being harrassed by a right-wing veterans' group for having a "Communist" choreographer. Then the company's prima ballerina is murdered onstage, and we are treated to pages of superb satire about professional dancers and their hangers-on and much tedious speculation about homicidal motives, interspersed with two more gruesome deaths.

Death Before Bedtime (1953) finds Peter in Washington as public relations adviser to an ultra-conservative senator angling for the presidential nomination--until he's blown to bits by a gunpowder charge in his fireplace. Once again a lackluster detective plot is saved by Vidal's mocking gibes at politics, journalism, sex and society. And in *Death Likes It Hot* (1954) Peter is invited to a weekend house party at a Long Island beachfront mansion and encounters tangled emotions and murder among a cast of ludicrous plutocrats and talentless pseudo-artists. Its fairly complex plot, a few deft clues and a dramatic climax make this the best mystery of the trio, but as usual it's the pungent satire that brings the book to life.

Clever deductions, fair play with the reader and the Agatha Christie-Ellery Queen bag of tricks are not Vidal's strong points. But his mastery of the language does not fail him even in these mysteries that he himself regarded merely as potboilers, and his tone of cynical good-humored tolerance towards an America populated exclusively by crooks, opportunists and buffoons is the closest thing to the authentic spirit of H. L. Mencken that readers of mystery fiction are ever likely to encounter. (Mike Nevins)

Edward D. Hoch, *The Thefts of Nick Velvet* (Mysterious Press, $10.00).

If ever there was a member of an endangered species it's Edward D. Hoch, the sole surviving professional writer of mystery short stories. Since his debut in 1955 and in addition to five novels he has published nearly 500 such tales, including numerous non-series stories and 15 separate series.

Among his recurring characters are an occult detective who claims to be two centuries old, a private eye, a Western drifter who may be the reincarnation of Billy the Kid, a priest, a British cryptographer-sleuth, an American police captain, a science-fictional Computer Investigation Bureau, a con man, two Interpol agents, a Lollipop Cop, and a New England physician-detective of the 1920s.

One of Hoch's longest running and most popular series

characters is Nick Velvet, a professional thief who restricts himself to stealing only unusual or valueless objects, charges his clients a minimum of $20,000 for his services, and is often forced to turn detective and solve some bizarre crime puzzle in the midst of his thieving. To date a total of 33 Velvet capers have been published--all but three in *Ellery Queen's Mystery Magazine*--and many have been reprinted in anthologies. (Five Velvets have been filmed and televised in France, but the American networks have consistently turned down a Velvet series on the ground that Nick is, after all, a thief who is never punished. Such a concept is acceptable here only if, like Robert Wagner in the "It Takes a Thief" series, the crook works for the government.)

Like Nick himself, The Mysterious Press specializes. Under the editorial direction of Otto Penzler, the Press concentrates on publishing collections of mystery short stories, largely because no other publisher will accept such collections in today's market. Fortunately Penzler has proved by success that books of short mysteries do and will sell, and his Press is growing at a steady pace.

The present collection, like all Mysterious Press offerings, is a superior specimen of the bookmaker's craft and the mystery writer's skill. In these 13 stories, first published between 1966 and 1975, Nick is hired to steal a zoo tiger, the water in a swimming pool, a baseball team, a sea serpent, a load of trash.

In one tale the puzzle is that he has to deduce what it is in a totally empty room that he was meant to steal, and in another what is stolen is Nick himself.

The stories are written in the plainest nuts-and-bolts style, but the ideas are generally stimulating, the plotting devious, and the best of these capers are neat miniaturizations of the kind of fair-play detective novels for which Ellery Queen whose magazine published them is famous. (Mike Nevins; this review and the one before are reprinted from the St. Louis *Globe-Democrat*.)

"*Death on the Nile*--Leisurely Peril", a film review by Donald A. Yates.

Hercule Poirot rides again! The last time (1974) it was a memorable journey on the Orient Express, wherein the shrewd Belgian detective was impersonated by British actor, Albert Finney. Now we have another Poirot--Peter Ustinov--who relives the detective's eventful excursion down the Nile aboard the luxury river steamer, "Karnak".

The new film, based on the late Agatha Christie's 1938 novel, is a vibrantly colorful travelogue whose early scenes laid in England are as visually pleasing as the long second segment filmed in Egypt. The puzzle element is also attractively managed and adheres very closely to the elaborate plot of the original novel. This makes for some fairly slow-moving sequences in the movie, when all efforts seem bent on advancing the formal investigation into the murder on board the "Karnak" of the beautiful but distressingly unpopular millionairess Linnet Doyle.

Progress is considerably inhibited by the presence on the "Karnak" of some half-dozen genuine suspects, all of whom have motives for doing in the victim, who was honeymooning with her handsome new husband on the Nile.

Yet the mystery is perplexing enough to keep the audience interested. And, after a while, as the bodies start accumu-
(continued on page 50)

THE DOCUMENTS IN THE CASE

(Letters)

From Bob Briney, 4 Forest Avenue, Salem, Massachusetts 01970: Your reduced tariffs for letter writers makes this the bargain of the century, and one that obviously loses you money that you could put to good use. We are all in your debt. ¶ V2n6 was packed with information and entertainment, as usual, and was enhanced by a fine printing job; no split rating this time! ¶ The topic of "When Is This Stiff Dead?" was interesting and unusual. Some of the hypothetical dialogue reminds me of my favorite line on the subject: Dion Fortune's reference to a mysterious figure glimpsed in the distance as "merely a corpse who was insufficiently dead". It is the "merely" that does the trick. ¶ A recently published bibliography of science fiction author Jack Vance contributes a tidbit to the continuing debate over who wrote certain "Ellery Queen" novels. The bibliography credits Jack Vance as the author of three of the EQ paperbacks of the mid-1960s: *The Four Johns* (1964), *The Madman Theory* (1966), and *A Room to Die in* (1965). A note asserts that a̶l̶l̶ three books were "rewritten by the publishers". There is also a disclaimer to the effect that "Mr. Vance does not acknowledge authorship of these Ellery Queen titles and therefore our source of information must be kept confidential." ¶ Do you think there is any possibility of squelching the barbarism "zine"? A publication like TMF is just as much a "magazine" or "journal" as any periodical with wider circulation and acceptance; it should not have to bear the belittling burden (even if no disparagement was intended) of the abbreviated term. (Perhaps my objection has a primarily esthetic basis: "zine" is such an *ugly* neologism!) [*As you will have seen from my editorial comments, I cannot take credit for the printing improvement. ¶ As for squelching "zine", I think it would be a losing cause--which is certainly no reason not to try. I agree that it is ugly, though not as much so as maga, and it does carry with it a connotation, deliberate or not, of inferiority. I think my nearly unconscious acceptance of it arose from the fact that I first encountered it in the form of fanzine, meaning a magazine for fans, and since fanzine was an artificial construct I was not so disturbed by its dismemberment as I would have been had I conceived of the corruption arising directly from magazine. Actually, however, the word magazine itself is, in its literary meaning, a relative newcomer to our language, having (I recall reading somewhere recently) first been applied to* Gentleman's Magazine *in the 18th century, and, as I have remarked before in these pages,* Blackwood's Edinburgh Magazine *was calling itself* Maga *in the early 19th century. Personally, my greatest objection to "zine" is that it smacks of the "in" words and phrases and gestures which adolescents of all ages use to demonstrate to each other that they are "with it", whatever that means. Frankly, the word [sic] embarrasses me in much the same way that I was recently embarrassed when I was introduced to a young man who insisted on going through a series of hand manipulations that would have put to shame a member in good standing of the Benevolent and Protective Order of Aphids, or any of the other fraternal orders which place so much importance on secret handclasps and the like. What, for God's sake, is wrong with a simple, straightforward handshake? Hell, I even still remove my glove when shaking hands, but it's been a long time since I've seen anyone else do it. I guess I'm just an old fogy. But, to get back to the point, Bob, your comments have called me back to my duty and I shall henceforth endeavor to refrain from encouraging, through example, the use of the corruption.]*

From Jon Breen, 10642 La Bahia Ave., Fountain Valley, CA 92708
I enclose my check for $3 for another year of *The MYSTERY FANcier*, wishing you and it a happy 1979. I feel a little sheepish about getting so much subscription credit for such short little letters. I will take it but will also try to comment at a little greater length this time around. ¶ I enjoyed David Doerrer's article about the Hon. Con. While I consider myself a fan of Joyce Porter, I don't enjoy her obnoxious female character nearly as much as I do her two obnoxious male characters, Dover and spy Eddie Brown. The reason is that the Hon. Con. represents a minority (in this case, lesbian) stereotype, and such are always somewhat distasteful. (I'll admit raising a question of good taste when discussing the works of Joyce Porter is itself pretty funny.) ¶ I share Marv Lachman's disapproval of the tendency of detective stories to have climaxes based on action rather than reason. Pure physical action--fights, chases, beatings--is the part of a book I am most apt to skip. (for a book that delivers first-rate action and deduction, no one should miss Mike Nevins's *Corrupt and Ensnare*.) ¶ The Nero Wolfe TV movie with Thayer David was shown at the second International Crime Writers' Congress in New York last spring. I don't know if it will ever be shown on TV, but it is mainly interesting as a curiosity, not as a good dramatic equivalent of the Wolfe novels. David could have been a pretty good Wolfe (though I didn't think he was fat enough for the role), but in the film he does some very unWolfean things, such as roaring with laughter at the end. By the way, I am one of those who feel the part of Wolfe so well suited to Orson Welles that it could have been written for him. *[Possibly David took the roar of laughter from the Sidney Greenstreet, radio version of Wolfe. I'm a bit embarrassed about mentioning this, but I have always felt that Jackie Gleason's face was excellent for the role, but I confess to having formed my opinion of Wolfe's actual appearance from the small portrait which appeared on the Bantam paperback editions of his adventures. I have never been able to see any actor in the role of Archie Goodwin; I suspect that's because I think Archie looks just like me.]*

From Marv Lachman, 34 Yorkshire Drive, Suffern, NY 10901:
Enclosed, out of a chaotic household, is my latest "It's About Crime" column. We're moving on January 12, and I felt that if I didn't write it now, I never would with all the things facing me. One of the things I'm looking forward to is enough space for all three thousand of my books. They're coming out of the closet. ¶ Another fine issue of TMF was Vol. , No. 6. I especially enjoyed Ms. Grochowski's article on Bouchercon. Because of economics and health, I missed my first Bouchercon since 1973. However, a combination of her article and a long letter from an old friend (and one of your subscribers), John Nieminski, was the next best thing to being there. ¶ Martin Morse Wooster seemed to think I was defending Ellery Queen on the question of who wrote those damned paperback originals. I suggest he reread my letter in the

prior issue. Doing that with perhaps some legal advice (are you there Mike Nevins?) might convey what I was trying to say.

From Don Cole, 15355 Mason Plaza, Omaha, Nebraska 68154:
I am sorry my contributions were so poor in the year 1978. You can be assured that I have read everything written and TMF continues to grow in stature. The Steve Lewis reviews are outstanding. "The Documents in the Case" are the best of any zine I've seen. And I thoroughly enjoy the editorial comments of the editor. He tells it like it is. ¶ It was good to see another letter from Judge-lawyer-writer Joe Hensley. Too little has been said about Hensley and his usual series hero Donald Roback. Hensley's books aren't hard sell types of mysteries but the kind you can crawl into on a cold winter's day and lose yourself. Personally I think his best was *Legislative Body* in which Roback is elected to his state's legislature. Hensley himself was once a member of the Indiana house and the experience made for a fine mystery. ¶ Late 1978 has brought us a couple of fine new authors and at least three superlative new mysteries. I haven't seen them reviewed yet in TMF but suppose Lewis will have them soon. I am anxious to see if he sees them as such excellent efforts as I have indicated. *Falling Angel* by William Hjortsberg (Harcourt Brace Jovanovich, 1978) is one of the strangest mysteries I have ever read. One of the most original and scary cop novels I have read in many years. Harry Angel is a tough and competent private eye who must delve into the supernatural. The ending may irritate you or amaze you but will certainly shock you. Fred Zackel's *Cocaine and Blue Eyes* (Coward McCann & Geoghegan, 1978) is about a licensed P.I. in San Francisco and again is an original. Kind of a modern day Dashiell Hammett in action. You've got it all in *Cocaine*, including a tour of Chinatown, the drug scene, Fisherman's Wharf and North Broadway. It's a long but fast paced book well handled and the conclusion is more than satisfactory. Elmore Leonard has written well in the past but his *Unknown Man No. 89* is by far his best to date. (Delacorte Press, 1977; Dell, 1978). Jack Ryan is back and just when you think you know this process server well he turns around and gives you a completely new look at his up and down personality. Lots of suspense and surprises in this one. Certainly one of the best I've read this year. And finally, more of a hair-raiser than a mystery is Brian Lecomber's *Talk Down* (Coward, McCann & Geoghegan, 1978). A young gal who has never been in a small plane before has her pilot-boyfriend become seriously ill and unable to fly the plane. She must rely on another pilot in the same type plane flying next to her to instruct her on how to get down. It's a plot that is similar to others but handled with great skill by the up and coming Lecomber.

From Mitch Grand, 2345 N. Second St., Harrisburg, PA 17110:
The first thing that caught my eye in the Table of Contents of Vol. 2, #6, was Amnon Kabatchnik's article on Agatha Christie. One of my favorite letter writers on my favorite author. Just great. And his title "A.C. is Still Alive and Well" is perfect. ¶ I've read Mary Ann Grochowski's "Benind the Scenes at Bouchercon 9" a half dozen times and always find something new to chuckle about. The Bismarck Hotel people acted like the Hotel Plaza in New York. And the Jeff and Jackie Meyerson party was so realistic I could almost taste the vodka martini. [*Wrong party. It was strictly beer out of cans and bourbon and scotch out of tooth glasses. Not a martini in sight.*] The David

Doerrer letter was almost "novella" length--but good! All in all--a fine issue. ¶ I suppose all mystery buffs have a favorite book store in their home towns, but we have one here in Harrisburg that is unique. Four and a half years ago Bob Marks opened a book store in the downtown section expecting to stay two months--and he's still here! And with good reason. The book store has no name and no bag to put your books in--but the prices and the personality of the owner are a joy. I suppose the majority of the books are ex-library books but they begin at $.50--and you can't top that. At first the books were mostly $.50 and $1.00--but now they go as high as $4.95. But you can't beat that. Some of the books are "hurt books", and some that I got for $.50 are *Audrey Rose*, *The World According to Garp*, *Fools Must Die*, *Death of an Expert Witness*, Mel Torme's *Wynner*, *Best Mystery Stories of 1978*, and a lot of Simenon's Maigret books. Makes your mouth water, doesn't it? Some days the owner sells everything for one dollar. Other days he'll give you a free book with each purchase. His hours are rather irregular. Some days he closes when he gets hungry. He isn't usually open on Saturday, but one Saturday when it was snowing he was open! Some days Bob has a caustic tongue and puts the people on--though most don't realize it. Bob says he finds the Harrisburg people "funny", but not too bright! I hope the $.50 bookstore stays as long as I'm around. I'd like to hear about the bocktores of your other writers.

From Jean-Jacques Schleret, 22, rue Ehrmann, 67000 - Strasbourg, France: Merci d'avoir laissé pour les souscripteurs étrangers l'abonnement à 12 dollars, bien que vous perdiez de l'argent. Si je peux vous rendre service en échange, n'hésitez pas. Je peux vous proposer un article sur "Donald Westlake/Richard Stark in the Movies". Si cela vous intéresse, dites-le moi, mais il faudra que vous traduisez cet article du français à l'américain. ¶ Pourrais-je demander à vos lecteurs dans "The Documents in the Case" du prochain TMF, si'ils ont des informations sur les auteurs de romans policiers suivants: Jerome Odlum; William O'Farrell; Day Keene; Raoul Whitfield; Thomas Walsh; et Lionel White. ¶ Ceci dit, votre revue est remarquable et contient pour le lecteur européen un quantité d'informations précieuses. Vous êtes sur la bonne voie! Longue vie à T.M.F. [*I would be delighted to have the Westlake/Stark article. Some years back I translated hundreds upon hundreds of letters, treaties and other documents for something I was writing at the time, and I found that translating from French to English was a damned sight more difficult than simply reading French with a fair degree of comprehension. But at least two of TMF's readers have the ability to translate from French to English with ease--Walter Albert is a professor of French, and Don Yates is a professor of romance Languages, so if Jean-Jacques' article shows up in these pages in the original French it will be because both of these fellows withheld their talents from the rest of us. Should that happen, I will supply you all with their home addresses, to which I hope you will post great volumes of hate mail. ¶ If anyone wants to respond to Jean-Jacques' request for information on the authors he lists, these pages are at your disposal--especially if the response is in the form of an article.*]

From Michael Doran, 4117 W. 90th Place, Hometown, IL 60456: Since I now seem to be in the thick of The Great Martin Morse Wooster Controversy (and if there's one thing I learned from reading Erle Stanley Gardner, it's to suspect anyone who always uses three names), I'd like to address myself to his latest and most astonishing utterance yet: to wit, that he "feels a duty to put the rumors on record, so that those who know can either prove or disprove them." Apparently, MMW is setting himself up as TMF's answer to Rona Barrett. Wooster is right when he says we're paying for *information*, but rumors are not information *unless they can be proven*. As to his having proven that one Queen book was not what it seemed, MMW has *proven* nothing; one conversation without documentation is not proof. Details of the events in question are what is required, and MMW, by his own admission, is not inclined to getting those details himself, preferring to let other TMFers do the hard work for him. In addition, MMW treats his speculations as if they are already accepted facts, which is, if I may resort to the vernacular, going about it bass-ackwards. If Wooster honestly believes that he has no obligation to back up his assertions *himself*, then he is not only deluding himself, but sabotaging his own credibility in the bargain. If I seem to be making prozine demands on Wooster (and indirectly on you as well), I'm sorry. No, dammit, I'm not sorry! Responsibility begins at home. Mr. Wooster, the ball's in your court: *you* prove your assertions, and I'll keep a carbon of this letter for eating. ¶ Perhaps I didn't make it clear that it was the reference to Gary Deeb that I wanted stricken from my last letter. I didn't think a Chicago local joke would go over with a specialized audience. Then again, Gary's brass prose is syndicated by the *Trib*, and unless I'm mistaken, Memphis is one stop on the route. Anyway, please clarify your intent: agreement, disagreement, or were you just trying to trick an explanation out of me. [*Yes*.] ¶ If it seems that I'm giving the rest of the issue short shrift, it's unintentional. I'm the type who never says a word unless I think I absolutely have to, and as you can see, I thought l'affaire Wooster was worth it. Keep up the good work.

From David Doerrer, 4626 Baywood Circle, Pensacola, FL 32504: A couple of additional comments on the index. Next year, you should arrange for 6 less reviews, or about 50 more! I hated to leave all that empty space on the last page. Of course, in pica it would be less as there would be a few more two-line entries. Have you ever played that child's game of repeating the same word over and over until it no longer looked as though it were spelled correctly? I began to feel that way about "Steve Lewis"! On the other hand, if Steve ever quits doing his monthly [*sic*] feature, and it is taken over by someone with a name like Albert Szent-Györgyi von Nagyrapolt, I might be less willing to do the index! You mentioned that you were aware that librarians did things differently, and they do in many instances. You have one in Janwillem van de Wetering. Assuming he is Dutch or Flemish, or at least from the Netherlands, the name should be entered under the part of the name following the prefix, i.e. Wetering, Janwillem van de. If he is actually English, or an expatriate Afrikaans, it should be entered under the prefix, regardless of the origin of the name in the latter case. It doesn't seem to have occurred to the linguistic geniuses who devised the rules for entry that the average patron who is only trying to find the book may neither know nor care what the author's national origin may have been. While we all know that the readers of TMF are far above average, I passed on the technicalities, and Janwillem is listed under van de Wetering, as he is referred to in the review. ¶ [. . . .] Mary Ann's article was delightful and really captured the spirit of Bouchercon. I didn't leave broke; I always hold out enough cash for a drink or two on the planes! In fairness to the Bismarck, I think I should mention that they did give us a ticket for a free drink (at least I got one). ¶ Really should have commented on "Mysteriously Speaking" first. Guy, I'd completely forgotten your incredibly generous policy of credit for contributions, and the fact that you count letters as such. My check is enclosed. I felt better when I got to the letters and saw that Martin had forgotten as well. ¶ Amnon Kabatchnik (you know, after the index I can now spell that without looking) and Marv Lachman have again turned out their usual polished efforts, and again managed to make them appear effortless, which I'm sure they weren't. Amnon, I was pleased to find out that you're a fellow Floridian. I'll try to give you a call the next time I'm in Tallahassee. Two small points. I seem to recall a review of *Agatha* which at least implied, if it didn't actually state, that this was neither respectable nor affectionate. While Dover's reprint of Thomson's *Masters of Mystery: A Study of the Detective Story* is certainly welcome, it isn't the first U.S. publication. Folcroft published a reprint in 1973. ¶ I also enjoyed "When Is This Stiff Dead?", especially for the quotations. ¶ A few (really) brief (honest) comments on the letters. Ellen, you're not using the same Rand-McNally I am. Nacogdoches is right there on p. 92 in F-12 (1975 ed.). See what a gullible sober-sides I am? I actually went and looked! Bill Crider and I have something in common (other than our low, and I'm sure wholly involuntary, interpretation of MFr); I liked *The Hanged Men* too. It may not have been great, or memorable, but for me it was "a good read". I also have to agree with Jeff Meyerson; no, I don't *have* to but it's a hackneyed expression I hate to give up. Martin needs far more than a casual conversation with Sturgeon to support his claim that he has "proved" that at least one of the Queen books wasn't written by Queen. Martin, I also think that you're a bit harsh on TAD re the subscription increase. The new rates did appear on the Table of Contents page in 11:3 and the explanation in 11:4. I grant that this doesn't constitute a personal message to subscribers in advance of the fact, but how many magazines do that? ¶ I seem to be all knocks and nit-picking this time, probably because, like the Chinese (I think I mean the Chinese) I've paid all my debts before the end of the old year and I'm broke and sour! Besides, if we all eulogized each other all the time, think how dull the letter column would become. ¶ I'll close on one last low blow. Guy, what is so hard about landing a plane after the pilot has had a heart attack? Matt Helm did it, the incredible Hulk did it, and even Charlie's Angels did it! Henceforth, all my mail is being vetted by a retired IRA bomb expert. [*A wise precaution, I'd say, if you plan to mention Charlie's Angels again in such close proximity to my name.*] ¶ A belated Happy New Year, everyone, and especially to Guy, who puts a lot more into TMF than many of us may realize. Best wishes for another great year!

From Jeff Banks, Box 3007 SFA Sta., Nacogdoches, TX 75962:

As 1984 draws nearer, it seems that a few of your constant readers are selecting others of us for the Orwellian honor of becoming "non-persons". When I join Marty Wooster on that list, I figure I'm in pretty good company. ¶ Of course, as your leadoff letter writer (E. Nehr) has discovered that I'm really your alter ego, we won't have to bother with another of these letters after this one. You'll have more time to devote more straightforwardly to the magazine since you won't have to busy yourself thinking up *bon mots* (carefully constructed as cues or lead-ins for your own topping remarks). ¶ Though I have thought of three more possible responses to Ms. Nehr's suggestion, I am going to be merciful and not say anymore about it. It does, however, since I have begun on the subject of letters, which I consciously try to say very little about, provide an excuse for dealing briefly with some of the others. Now that "my" apprevation for your publication has drawn a response, I'll stop using it. Undoubtedly, many of your readers caught the significance, but it took another Texan to almost match my crudity by commenting on it! Your own answers to the letters were, as always, the highpoint of the letter column; the best argument for continuing it as you do (whatever my preferences or those of any other reader). I honestly think you are the best editorial responder to letters since Sam Merwin (now ed. of *Mike Shayne's M.M.*) whose letter columns in *Startling Stories* and *Thrilling Wonder Stories* ("the Thrilling Twins", sci fi pulps) in the mid-late 1940s constituted high art. That comparison is the highest compliment I could think of. And I especially liked your remarks on where to place the punctuation in relation to quotation marks--it would seem that detective-mystery fans should be better able to appreciate logic than any other sizable group (philosophers/logicians excluded); your argument was a brilliant display of it. Dave Doerrer's monumental 5-pager is also a strong support for his defense of letters; I especially thank him for the index to contributors to *Murder Ink*. What I really most wanted to know was whether Spillane was one of the contributors, as I had enjoyed seeing him help Ms. Wynn hype the sale of the book last spring on Tom Snyder's *Tomorrow* show. That contributor list was enough work, covered enough space, and possibly was of interest enough to your readers that I think it should have been credited on *your* contents page. Finally, let me admit that most of the letters you run are not the kind that I object to. As long as they tell more than just what a particular reader liked (or didn't) in a particular issue, if they raise interesting questions or make sensible comments, then they are worthwhile. Still, mind you, far from my favorite part of any magazine, but definitely worthwhile! ¶ Enjoyed the Wolfe saga immensely, as usual. But since you have mentioned *The Great American Detective* didn't run the Wolfe yarn you recommended, perhaps you should tell us which one you wanted included. The editors ran my second choice for a Mike Shayne story; my first recommendation (rejected because of length) was the truly classic novelette "A Taste for Cognac". ¶ Seeing "When Is This Stiff Dead?" so quickly into print was a distinct pleasure. Let me remind you that I do need a couple of contributor off-prints. Also, I noted the prevalence of typos--much more than your usual quota, not only here but throughout the magazine. I attribute them to your concentration on achieving real excellence in printing, and I trust you'll have the number reduced again soon. Finally, regarding the charts: I have at last received *Last*

Day in Limbo (only 2 days before the latest *Fancier*), and if I can get around to it will finish up my Modesty Blaise chart to enclose with this. Have also managed to round up all but one of the Joaquin Hawks adventures, and once that is complete I'll put together a chart for the series. ¶ As usual, I enjoyed the articles, being especially glad that George Dove has finally joined your list of contributors. But I enjoyed the reviews most of all. This time Steve did include three reviews of private eye books (unfortunately all things I've already read), and the miscellaneous reviewers added another three. I noted that I and Steve didn't agree in our opinions any more than usual. Among the miscellaneous reviews, I especially liked Wooster's and the one by Joe Lansdale. My "Mystery +" column in *The Poisoned Pen* will treat *The Holmes-Dracula File* at greater length than Joe did sometime in 1979. ¶ Summing up your year, I can honestly say that the magazine continues to improve. You have set a standard of quality that you may find hard to match next year. ¶ Important Post Script: [*Honest, that what it says!*] When "When Is This Stiff Dead?" was presented at one of the many delightful "Mystery Sections" of the April 1978 national meeting of the Popular Culture Association, Mike Nevins pointed out that most states (possibly all) have legal machinery that works quite well at untangling the "who died first" wuestion which is central to the ending of the paper. That, of course, not only somewhat undercuts the cleverness of Smith's ending to *The Death of the Detective*, but also of the Thompson-Banks article. [*Thanks, Jeff, for the several high compliments you pay me. I am ver appreciative, though I suppose they will only reinforce Ellen Nehr's conviction that I am writing the letters over your c:gnature.* ¶ *When Steven Krauzer asked me to recommend one of the Nero Wolfe shorts for his anthology I was confronted with something of a problem, because I see the Saga as a continuing whole, the parts of which all intertwine, and asking me to specify the best episode is something like asking me to pick out a month in my life and designate it as my best month. (To completely demolish whatever logic the foregoing may contain, I should say that I have no difficulty at all pointing to my favorite novel--Some Buried Caesar, hands down.) Besides, I was only half through with my rereading of the Saga, and naturally I remembered those stories I had recently reread better than those I had read years before. Anyway, I recommended "Black Orchids", though I probably would have recommended something else had I already finished my rereading when I was asked. For more on the subject, se Stephen's letter below.* ¶ *My apologies for the excessive typos. Because of the time involved, I don't proofread the pages of TMF before they are printed, so if I don't catch a typo when I make it it doesn't get corrected. Too, it is almost impossible to correct errors neatly once the page has been rermoved from the typewriter.* ¶ *As for the improved quality of reproduction, see my remarks in "Mysteriously Speaking . . ."*]

From Steven Krauzer, 1300 Van Buren, Missoula, Montana 59801: I'm afraid your continual problems with the U.S. Postal Service have struck again, and as a result we're both the victims of a misunderstanding. ¶ The fact is that your letter in response to mine (in which I queried you as to suggestions for a Nero Wolfe to be included in *The Great American Detective*) never arrived. I was curious at the time about why you hadn't answered, but I suppose I assumed that you were just too tied up with moving, teaching, putting out TMF, etc. And I was pretty much under the gun at the time, shooting for a contract deadline that was beginning to seem like only a vague hope. So I never followed up. ¶ I'm sorry this happened. I certainly would have valued your suggestions. In any case, I'm glad you mentioned my failure to heed you, or else I would have never known what had happened. ¶ So, thanks for the plug in TMF II,6, and best wishes for continued success in all ventures for the new year.

From Randy Cox, Route 5, Box 10, Northfield, Minnesota 55057: After the first acidic reviews ot The Mystery Library in TMF I looked forward to any commnets on the volume to which I had made a modest contribution with some traits of masochism. While I am delighted that my high opinion of *The 39 Steps* is shared by your reviewer (though I wouldn't use the word "paranoid" in describing Buchan), which demonstrates he has some taste, I was surprised by his disbelief that the film version should be better known than the book. ¶ Mystery fans dedicated enough to support publications like TMF are in a minority among the general reading public. They are also better informed about the minutia of the genre and (to some extent) live in a world apart and speak little to mortals. I assure you, I have talked with a great many people who have never heard of either the book or the author who have seen the film. I am reminded of a *Punch* cartoon of recent date in which a man clutching a book and rolling his eyes to the heavens says to his wife: "Do you know, there are people in that office who have never read a Buchan." They sometimes mispronounce his name: it's Buck'an, *not* B*yoo*'kan. It is a sad state of affairs, of course. I remember surprising a student of English literature with the information that *Frankenstein* was a novel before it was a movie. Every year I teach students about Sherlock Holmes who think his real name was Rathbone and I'm still meeting people who don't know Conan Doyle wrote anything except Sherlock Holmes. ¶ You can't take anything for granted. ¶ The reviewer omitted one novel in listing sequels to *The 39 Steps--The Man from the Norlands* (British title: *The Island of Sheep*). Richard Hannay also appears in one short story in *The Runagates Club*. ¶ "Pompous" is hardly a word I would have used to describe Otto Penzler's style, but I guess your reviewer is qualified to judge. It takes one to . . . ¶ I can hardly wait for the verdict on *The Right Red Hand*, a book I can find almost nothing about in any of the many volumes of references on mysteries apart from the *Encyclopedia of Mystery and Detection*. It was included in the Dell Great Mystery Library and now is part of The Mystery Library. I guess it has to be a classic. ¶ I knew that H. R. F. Keating's *Agatha Christie, First Lady of Crime* was a good book, but do you realize it has been reviewed *three* times in TMF? [*No, I am chagrined to confess, it had escaped my attention until you pointed it out.*] Twice by Amnon Kabatchnik (2:1 and 2:6) and once by Marvin Lachman (2:5). I've noticed two reviews for a number of books in past issues, but *three*? Everybody! Go right out and . . . .

From Michael Cook, 3318 Wimberg Ave., Evansville, In 47712: Just a little advance note to you on the forthcoming publication of my latest book, *Murder by Mail; The History of the Mystery Book Clubs with Complete Checklist*. This is nearly complete and should be published in January, and will be a complete checklist of the Unicorn Mystery Book Club, the Detective Book Club, and The Mystery Guild, along with supplementary data on original publishers, original publisher's price, publication date of original (in regard to Mystery Guild titles), as well as history of each Club. I might add that the previous list of Unicorn titles published in 1975 in *The Armchair Detective* listed many of the books with the order of titles not in proper sequence which made it difficult for searchers to locate some. I myself had a list of DBC titles in an earlier issue of that same periodical, but the book will bring this up to date for that Club. As yet, price not determined, but I will keep you informed and see you receive a notice when ready.

Joe L. Hensley, 2315 Blackmore, Madison, Indiana 47250:
I enclose my check for another year. I'd like to subscribe to more fanzines, but I suppose I'll continue to hold it to yours and *The Poisoned Pen*. I subscribed to TAD for years and liked it very much, but the type was small enough to give me headaches so I stopped. ¶ For Michael Doran in case Mike Nevins doesn't get around to replying on the Nero Wolfe telefilm: One was shown at the International Crime Writers meeting in NYC in March of 1978. It drew a mixed reaction. I rather liked it. That meeting was truly great fun, something going on about every minute. I thought Mike Nevins was putting me on when he brought someone around who claimed to be a *Time* reporter. He wasn't kidding. There were cocktail parties at Brentanos, at Harper and Row, dinners, luncheons, lectures, panel discussions. The next one of these is in Stockholm in, I believe, 1981. The first one was in London in 1975. It was great also. A' the London meeting and at the one in New York there were a number of reader-fans in attendance. The easiest way to get the word on going to Stockholm would be by joining M.W.A. The address is, Mystery Writers of America, Inc., 105 E. 19th St. (#3D), New York, NY 10003. ¶ TMF 2/6 was up to its usual standards. I liked the Bouchercon 9 report and wish I could have attended. Some year maybe.

From Mike Nevins, 4466 W. Pine Blvd., #23-C, St. Louis, MO:
I have some very bad news for your readers. A week ago, on December 15, contributor Larry French lost control of his car while driving home at night and was killed instantly when the auto collided with a light pole. Larry edited his own mystery fanzine, *Culprit Confesses*, and was working on a book about his favorite detective writer, John Dickson Carr, He will be badly missed. ¶ In reply to Michael Doran's letter, a couple of years ago Putnam decided to drop its "Red Mask Mysteries" imprint and publish its mysteries without a category designation. This was in response to the then much-discussed death of the mystery novel and in the hope that without being categorized as such more mysteries might get on the best-seller lists. As for the Nero Wolfe pilot film, I saw it last March when it was screened at the Crime Writers' Congress and, believe me, you haven't missed much. ¶ Gerie Frazier is right in remembering that Bill Pronzini's "Jack Foxx" novel *Freebooty* first appeared as a magazine novelette. Specifically, it's in *Alfred Hitchcock's Mystery Magazine*, March 1974, as "The Riverboat Gold Robbery."

From Bill Crider, 4206 Ninth St., Brownwood, TX 76801:
TMF arrived today, just in time for Christmas. I want to set

Ellen Nehr straight, at least about Texas. It's true that there is not a Nacodgoches, Texas, but there *is* a Nacogdoches (which we central Texas boys pronounce Kak-ak-dō'-chiz, in order to avoid confusing it with the Louisiana town of Nachitoches, which we call Nak'-ah-tosh). I won't even ask how she looked in the lampshade. ¶ This leads me in a round-about way to Jeff Banks and his article done in collaboration with Leslie M. Thompson. I'd like to quote them a line from a paper written by a student of mine, which I believe is the last work on their topic. The student was writing about a poem by Thomas Hardy, but his comment seems to fit the article. His last sentence, and I'm quoting exactly, was, "When you is die, you is die." Just why I was trying to get a student who would write a sentence like that to appreciate the virtues of a poem by Thomas Hardy is another story, too long to go into here, but I'll have to admit that the sentence does have a certain succinct power. It might not satisfy Banks and Thompson, but I think you could make a good case for its accuracy. ¶ As usual in reading over the reviews, I spot books that I want to read and wonder why I've never seen them. I keep a pretty close watch on the newsstands; why haven't I seen *Stud Game*? Doesn't Pocket Books like Texans? I also spot reviews that I want to agree with, such as Joe Lansdale's of *The Holmes-Dracula File*. Maybe not all your readers enjoy the Count as much as I do, but for those who do I'd like to recommend Fred Saberhagen's earlier paperback (Warner, 1975), which is really a "prequel" to this latest one. The title is *The Dracula Tape*; it re-tells Bram Stoker's tale in the Count's own words, and it shows that Stoker was a prejudiced stretcher of the truth. ¶ Mary Ann Grochowski's report on the Bouchercon made me wish more than ever that I'd been there.

From Joe Lansdale, Route 8, Box 231, Nacogdoches, TX 75961: Enjoyed the latest *Mystery Fancier*, as usual. But, pardner, when you call me a *gastard*, smile. Uh . . . what's a gastard? ¶ Anyway, gastard or not, I'm glad you got that Jeff Banks stuff cleared up and it's Mertz that's the nice guy and not Jeff. Jeff, now put that autographed Mike Hammer .45 down... just ajokin'. ¶ Very glad Jeff mentioned *The Not So Private Eye*, which is a hell of a lot of fun and a boon to us long suffering private eye fans . . . hear me suffering (weep, gnash of teeth, pain in the lower right leg). Also liked Jeff's article with Thompson. I remember when Jeff was planning it and looking for references to dead folks in detective novels. I humored him, but I don't believe I ever found anything to help him. Maybe I loaned him the John Ball book. ¶ Nice to read about Bouchercon. Would love to go to one of those, but it'll have to be closer to good old Nacogdoches-- Yes, Ellen Nehr, id does exist, oldest town in Texas and I'll have to have some money. However, it sounds like they had a lot of fun without me. ¶ Loved the letter section and didn't mind the long letter Doerrer was worried about. As I've said before, I like the letter section. I think a lot of folks will write a letter of comment where they might not attempt an article. Or might not have the time for one. (Where the hell do Jeff Banks and Steve Lewis get all the time? Answer: They make it. Maybe that should tell the rest of us something.) ¶ One minor complaint: Man, is the print strained, or maybe my baby greys are just low on batteries. Or maybe I got a turkey copy--you wouldn't send the old sarcastic gastard a turkey copy on purpose, would you? [*Who, me?*] ¶ Whatever, by the time I finished reading TMF my eyes were in a hell of a strain. But, if it takes print that small--and sometimes blurry--to give us the meat you give us, so be it. Personally, I don't mind the price raise, and you shouldn't really give a damn if anyone does. It may be *our* magazine, but *you're* the one that has to pay to have it printed and mailed. ¶ Odds and ends: Enjoyed the article by Dove and Grochowski's Bouchercon report which I've already mentioned. Lewis's reviews as always, and agreed whole heartedly with Doerrer's comments on violence, but since I've written on that before, even got on my soap box once about it, I'll refrain. Would like to know if anyone out there has a copy of Finney's *Time and Again* for sale. I loved *The Body Snatchers* and mystery-science fiction is a favorite of mine. ¶ Just saw the movie *Magic*, and although I felt it promised much more than it delivered, it was faithful to the book in form, if not in tension. Not an altogether satisfying movie, but interesting, and Hopkins was marvelous.

From Jeff Meyerson, 50 1st Place, Brooklyn, NY 11231:
This Martin Wooster business is really getting out of hand. I know Martin is trying to be controversial (he's said so many times, including in person). Nevertheless, I really wish he would refrain from making statements like "I've proved that at least one book attributed to Queen was not, in fact, written by them." The only possible answer to this is, OH YEAH? NOT TO ME YOU HAVEN'T! First of all, I don't know how many of Queen's books Martin has read. I have not read them all, but I have read more than half, and I have no doubts in my mind that Dannay and Lee *did* write *The Player on the Other Side*. To convince me otherwise Martin will have to offer some real proof, not unsubstantiated claims by a not disinterested party. (Proof--"the process or an instance of establishing the validity of a statement esp. by derivation from other statements in accordance with accepted or stipulated principles of reasoning"--Webster's 7th New Collegiate Dictionary.) I recommend Mike Nevins' superb *Royal Bloodline* to Martin to study before he "proves" anything else about Queen. As far as the Tim Corrigan and other paperback series books "signed" by Queen, there is no doubt that these *were* ghostwritten. I can't remember all the names I've heard in connection with this business, but Richard Deming was one. Personally, I find this whole practice of putting out these books under the "Ellery Queen" name bad taste to say the least, even false advertising. ¶ Another item of interest to me this time was George Dove's piece on the cop abroad. It is an interesting idea for an article, and several other examples come to mind, including Simenon's *Maigret in New York's Underworld* and Marric(Creasey)'s *Gideon's Badge* (also in New York). Can anyone think of others? I just did--how about George Bagby's excellent *The Body in the Basket*? (It's set in Madrid.)

From Carla J. Fisher, 10757 Evanston North, Seattle, WA 98133:
I'm afraid I may have misunderstood but, as I was consuming the back issues of TMF, I was astounded to find, in volume 2, number 3, that you mention starting an amateur publication association. Do you really mean that you would provide an outlet for people writing mystery fiction with opportunity for feedback from other writers? If such is the case, I would very much like to be a part of that endeavor. I've been sitting here praying for something of the sort and think you're

magnificent for offering to make it a reality. ¶ Whether or not the majority of your subscribers are male chauvanists, I am happy to have obtained copies of your publication (though I'm missing much of volume one) and find TMF quite enlightening. [...] ¶ I am still interested in obtaining the balance of back issues. Perhaps you could put a blurb in the letters section of your mag. in case someone has the copies I want and would be willing to part with them, or let me copy them. I already have: November, 1976; September 1977; November, 1977; January, 1978 through September, 1978, so the ones I need are the first numbers of volume one. [*See my remarks in "Mysteriously Speaking . . ."--if I remember to make them.*] ¶ I notice that you request artwork for your covers and will see if I can come up with something. You're wonderful to provide such a fine outlet for creative thought. ¶ Please let me know of any developments toward the apa and I will try to comply. [*The amateur publication association which I, in a fit of insanity, offered to start last year never came to anything. Only two people expressed the slightest interest, and I soon realized that I didn't have the time to take on such a project. However, there already is an amateur publication association for mystery fans--DAPA-EM--and a sample mailing can be had by sending a dollar to Art Scott, 10365 Wunderlich Drive, Cupertino, CA 95014.*]

From Gerie Frazier, 415 Sage Hills St., Apt. B, Rawlins, WY: What's up? Is Ellen Nehr trying to stir up a controversy over Jeff Banks such as others have over Martin Wooster? Being an alter ego for Guy M. Townsend, that is. Fie!! ¶ Being a Texan-by-marriage, I've known of Nacogdoches for many years. It is indeed known to Rand-McNally, appearing in their road atlas, 53rd annual edition, 1977. Page 92 thereof, between markers 12 and 13 at top of the page, and nearly even with marker F at the right hand side of page. ¶ This fine city has at least one claim to fame--several football players from Nacogdoches have been chosen to be members of the AP All-America Football Team; the most recent such player was introduced on the Bob Hope Christmas Show which was shown in our area on December 22, 1978. ¶ Also, how could Ellen have overlooked previous letters written to TMF by Joe Lansdale, another resident of Nacogdoches? ¶ Okay, it was easy enough to prove the existence of the town--is there really a Jeff Banks? Having a tinge of amateur sleuth in my nature, I dialed 555-1212 and was given a telephone number for Jeff Banks, so it appears certain that he is "alive and breathing the air of Nacogdoches, Texas". ¶ Am looking forward to Ellen's promised article for Volume 3. Her letters have been well written and humorous, so the article should be very interesting. ¶ TMF 2:6 is about the best to date in my opinion. Splendid articles, and a quick glance at the reviews indicated I'd better MAKE the time to read them. A very Happy New Year to our friendly editor, and to all subscribers!

From Jane Gottschalk, 611 A Franklin St., Oskosh, WI 54901: When I returned from the Christmas holidays, I found 2:6 of TMF awaiting me--with its goodies to read and its reminder that subscription payments are due. Ergo, my check for $9.00 is enclosed. ¶ That issue was another example of the enthusiasm and energy of its editor (the best printed to date), its contributors and its subscribers. And it glowed with agape reminiscences of Bouchercon 9. Can you bear yet another recollection? When you were circulating, with camera slung with a wide colorful band around neck, you approached John McAleer and me and generously extended an invitation to an "after" party. We were exchanging stories about *The New Yorker* (heretical behavior for the evening?) to which he also contributes, and when you left, he said: "Good heavens! I thought he was coming to give me absolution and I didn't know what I had done wrong!'" (I take issue with your counter stand against the style sheets' recommendations about punctuation marks and quotation marks and placement thereof. They are standardized conventions--as much as spelling. Private *eyes* can make for entertaining reading, but that of private *I's* can be deplorably egocentric.) To return to that evening. I was very sorry that I was not able to accept your invitation; I had to be up--and away--early the next day, so that I also missed the Sunday morning session. I hoep that you wrote, or found someone to write, another version of the weekend. I thoroughly enjoyed Mary Ann Grochowski's personal glimpses of people, written, as usual, with her bright spirits. ¶ To put a stop to your grand masquerade:

      The *MYSTERY FAncier*'s ed,
      For subbers has blithesomely bled.
      And he *is* quite a guy,
      With no Squint in the eye,
      A tallie who looks underfed.

[*I'm afraid the "looks underfed" is a bit of poetic license on Jane's part.*]

From Bob Adey, 7 Highcroft Ave., Wordsley, Stourbridge, West Midlands, DY8 5LX, England: The last 10 days have brought copies of TMF, *Poisoned Pen* and *The Not So Private Eye*, so things are looking up. ¶ Wooster's comments in TMF 2:5 on the Uncle Abner stories are most interesting. I have always thought the stories of exceptional quality but overrated to the extent that I would not go along with Queen's inclusion of them as one of the "big four", the other three being Poe, Doule and Chesterton. In fact there is even a doubt in my mind whether the Father Brown saga quite measures up to Holmes and Dupin. ¶ Jeff Banks' letter has started me thinking about missing art objects, manuscripts etc. (and those about to be discovered). Marco Page's *Reclining Figure*, Barnaby Ross' *Drury Lane's Last Case*, John Evans' *Halo for Satan* (a manuscript in the hand of Christ, no less), Robert Robinson's *Landscape With Dead Dons*--all of them come somewhere near the mark. ¶ I find it difficult to believe that Ellery Queen did not write some of the later novels, particularly *The Finishing Stroke* and *Face to Face*, both so typical (I would have said) of Queen at his best. If they were not written by the genuine team, I'd certainly like to know who did write them, so that I can track down their other books! ¶ Does anyone know a book called *Death Under the Table* by South African author Peter Godfrey. It may well have had an American distributor and Bill Dunn certainly sold a copy recently (but can't remember to whom). Can anyone help? ¶ Finally, has my subscription run out yet (or is it about to?). I'll make the next one airmail I think to give myself a better chance of joining in with the discussions nearer to the time of publication of TMF. [*Second letter:*] Had to come into a second letter because I forgot to say the one thing that I was determined to say. Jeff Meyerson has spoken most kindly of his visit to England and the hospitality offered by both Neville Wood and myself (or more correctly my wife). ¶ I feel that on behalf of both Neville and myself the other side must also be stated. Jeff and Jackie are really the most pleasant house guests that you could wish for. Furthermore on behalf of Sue and myself I must say that when we visited New York (all too briefly) in Spetember Jeff and Jackie were equally as good hosts to us as we were to them. ¶ I'm writing to tell you this because I don't imagine for one minute that, if I wrote to Jeff and told him, he'd publish one blooming word of it. Modest so and so.

From Helen D. Weber, 726 E. Pierce St, Phoenix, AZ 85006: It was only last November 10 that I sent a check for a subscription to *The MYSTERY FANcier*, and what an interesting group of people I have met through its pages, and what nice things have occurred since then. I became aware of the 'zine through a plug in EQMM. It was the mention of the Nero Wolfe Saga which motivated me. ¶ One of my four retirement projects was to obtain and reread my old time favorites in the mystery field. I started out with trying to obtain Dorothy Sayers, Agatha Christie, John Dickson Carr, and Nero Wolfe. I was fairly easily successful in the first two, but I'm having a lot of difficulty with the latter two. My wish was to save them until I could read them in the order they were written. ¶ By the time my check arrived in November, v. 1, #1-4 were out of print. Therefore, my first thanks go the the benefactor who allowed me to have xeroxed these missing issues. I appreciate it very much. Since I cannot reciprocate the favor to my benefactor, perhaps I can make an offer to those two readers who were seeking v. 1, #1 to have that issue xeroxed for them. ¶ The second very nice thing that happened was that Carl Kutzner xeroxed and sent to me the article and check list for the DBC which appeared in *The Armchair Detective*, v. 8, #2. He also included a different and very helpful listing from *The Mystery Nook*. He has been recompensed for the cost, but for his time and kindness, I am in his debt. I shall keep in mind his want-list of DBCs, should I ever come across them. ¶ My thanks to Elinor Portser for the address for Dover Books. I have received the catalog and have happily ordered six of the titles including *The Mystery of the Yellow Room*, which I have never read and have heard mentioned many times. Incidentally, I have five Dovers which I ordered from the Publisher's Central Bureau. Sorry I can't give the address, but I will save it the next mailing I get from them, and they arrive very frequently. Their mystery list is quite small and of course variable, but I have obtained some good titles from them. One of the Dovers I got from them is King: *The Curious Mr. Tarrant*. It is not listed in the current Dover catalog, so it must be out of print already. ¶ Does anyone know where the U.S. office of Penguin is? [*Viking/Penguin, Inc., 625 Madison Ave., New York, NY 10022.*] I wrote to an address that I found somewhere. I believe it was a Maryland address, but the letter was returned. ¶ Now for some of the interesting people I have met through the pages of the 'zine. My first salute goes to kindred spirit Ellen Nehr. I too am a HIBK. We seem to be a minority of a minority within a minority. Let's form a cell and bore from within. [*I trust that my heroic restraint in not commenting on the juxtaposition of "HIBK" and "bore" has not gone unnoticed.*] Our first project will be to hang Martin Wooster in effigy next Guy Fawkes day,

I in Arizona and you in Ohio, for his review of *The Circular Staircase*. Since you have actually met him Ellen, give me a description. Look, Junior! *The Circular Staircase* was written in 1908, as you noted yourself. One must read books within the time they are written. This was a mystery then (and it is now, for that matter) but it was not a detective novel. In her day, Mary Roberts Rinehart was one of the most popular novelists in America. ¶ I enjoyed your letters on collecting, Ellen. By the way, you can find Nacogdoches, Texas in the zip code directory. I too failed to find it in Rand McNally, a road map of Texas, or the WPA guide to Texas, but there really is a Nocogdoches, and its zip really is 75601. [*I might lie about somethings, but never about a zip code.*] ¶ Greetings to fellow-sufferers at the Library of Congress: John Nieminski and David Doerrer. John never went back the second time. I did go back once, but only to take a visiting nephew to see the Declaration of Independence. David, I also first visited LC as a young librarian with only a couple of years experience, and my reaction was the same as yours. However, my visit was in the early 40's as opposed to yours in 1969. I was very interested in your comments concerning the attempt to improve conditions. I am a subscriber to LC Card Division for use with my Arizona collection, so I do still receive their catalog bulletin, but I miss receiving other information. ¶ Hello to Judity Fiene (2:3, 73) who doesn't enjoy short stories. I agree. That's why I don't read EQMM in its entirety. I do read the reviews and comment and look for the longest story in the issue. That's also why the only Mystery Library volume I left unfinished was *The Complete Uncle Abner*. Our circle here is made up of four retired women who share our books. They end up here, where they go into a storage room fitted up with book shelves. When *Uncle Abner* gets back, I shall continue reading him, but only a few at a time. One of our foursome subscribes to EQMM, so it does get into my hands, and I do enjoy parts of it very much. ¶ To Nero Wolfe, Guy Townsend, and several others who are bothered because the English language needs a third pronoun; look, there is just such a word. Let's quote from a letter from Jane Bakerman (2:2, 42): "But I think that shouldn't stop *anyone* who is really "into" mystery/detective fiction from setting down her/his comments and sending them in. A perceptive reader is a perceptive reader, and what she/he has to say . . . " Let's do these two sentences this way: "But I think that shouldn't stop *anyone* who is really 'into' mystery/detective fiction from setting down one's comments and sending them in. A perceptive reader is a perceptive reader, and what one has to say . . . ." "One" may sound affected at first, but let's all get used to it, and stop all of this nonsense of the he/she. [*"One" is indeed awkward, and, since writers will continue to use he except when a woman is referred to, its use would be a sure tip off as to the sex of the "one". Besides, It is my hope that when the hysteria of this women's liberation thing dies down somewhat, literate people of both sexes will acknowledge that there never was anything "sexist"--God help me, the words this thing has led to!--about using "he" or "chairman" or other words of that type. And please--don't anyone tell me that hysteria is a sexist word! There's just so much of this garbage I can take.*] ¶ Since Dorothy Glantz left the fold (2:1, 55), are there any more such ardent feminists out there? Not me, but I did get a chuckle out of Jane's turning the tables with her she/he rather than the usual he/she. ¶

Guy, somebody has to defend Martin Wooster in his use of Library of Congress capitalizations of titles. LC rule is that the first word and only proper nouns are capitalized. I am enclosing two LC cards as examples. I, myself, have arrived at the use of all capital letters for titles. This eliminates quotation marks, or underlining, and deciding which capitalization form one shall use. I notice that Jeff Meyerson used the same form for his index for volume 1. [*What form librarians use on their card catalogue entries has nothing to do with the proper form in books and periodicals such as TMF. A quick glance at the Wilson Library Bulletin shows me that in that publication, written by and for librarians, the conventional practice of capitalization in titles is observed, not the one you and Martin advocate. As for the practice of writing out titles in all caps, it does save time--but so does leaving out all punctuation. For indices and such I acknowledge its convenience and permit it in these pages; otherwise, italics or underlinings are the correct form.*] ¶ As to all you other contributors, reviewers, and letter writers, you are all interesting persons. Mostly, my thanks to Guy for a new and interesting experience in my introduction to FANdom. ¶ PS: It occurred to me that it might be apropos to state that of the four of us avid "whodunit" readers, not one of our husbands is interested. Two of our husbands are not only readers but collectors. One of us is a widow, but we know her husband was a reader and also a collector. The fourth husband--alas! --has made a very poor adjustment to retirement, and spends the whole day with TV. ¶ Now it occurs to me that it might be interesting to query your readers to find out how many of their wives also read our 'zine. I honestly think that you will find that the proportion is much greater than 80% vs. 20%. [*Mine doesn't.*]

www.ingramcontent.com/pod-product-compliance
Lightning Source LLC
Chambersburg PA
CBHW031427040426
42444CB00006B/713